FRENCH INSTITUTIONS

Values and Politics 834

by Saul K. Padover

with the collaboration of

François Goguel

Louis Rosenstock-Franck

Eric Weil

Hoover Institute Studies

STANFORD UNIVERSITY PRESS

This is one of a group of four related studies on French politics and society planned for the Hoover Institute Studies. This group also includes a study of national character by Rhoda Métraux and Margaret Mead, and two studies of French political symbolism and elites by Daniel Lerner and the RADIR staff. These, together with Mr. Padover's study of French political institutions and values, may give the reader an overview of the dynamics of modern France as a participant in the world political community.

Dean Padover's volume, worked out in collaboration with three prominent French scholars, surveys the conflicting values in the traditions of the French Revolution and French conservatism. It then examines what has happened to these values under the impact of twentieth-century social problems, war, and defeat.

This study was initiated as part of the RADIR Project (Revolution and the Development of International Relations), of which Mr. Padover was a consultant.

HOOVER INSTITUTE STUDIES

Series E. Institutions, No. 2   April 1954

FRENCH INSTITUTIONS

Values and Politics

by Saul K. Padover

with the collaboration of

François Goguel

Louis Rosenstock-Franck

Eric Weil

The Hoover Institute and Library
on War, Revolution, and Peace
Stanford University

STANFORD UNIVERSITY PRESS

THE HOOVER INSTITUTE STUDIES

This series of studies undertakes to describe the world revolution of our time and its consequences for world politics and national policy. These studies were conducted by the Hoover Institute and Library of War, Revolution, and Peace as part of its research project on Revolution and the Development of International Relations (RADIR Project).

The studies and their publication were made possible by funds granted by Carnegie Corporation of New York. That Corporation is not, however, the author, owner, publisher, or proprietor of this publication, and it is not to be understood as approving by virtue of its grant any of the statements made or views expressed therein.

Harold H. Fisher, Chairman of the Hoover Institute
C. Easton Rothwell, Director of the Hoover Institute
Daniel Lerner, Director of Research
Ithiel de Sola Pool, Assistant Director of Research

STANFORD UNIVERSITY PRESS
STANFORD, CALIFORNIA

Printed in the United States of America
by Stanford University Press

Library of Congress Catalog Card Number: 53-11875

Star crucified— by traitors sold,
Star panting o'er a land of death, heroic land,
Strange, passionate, mocking, frivolous land.

Miserable! yet for thy errors, vanities, sins,
    I will not now rebuke thee.
Thy unexampled woes and pangs have quell'd them all,
And left thee sacred.

— Walt Whitman, O Star of France (1870 — 71)

France is too high minded, has too much innate
force, intelligence and elasticity, to remain under
its present compression. Samson will arise in his
strength, as of old.

— Thomas Jefferson, in 1816

TABLE OF CONTENTS

I. BASIC VALUES OF FRENCH CIVILIZATION*

As a starting point one can take the French Revolution— the "revolution that failed" or the "victory that was lost"—to be the historic event that determined, or crystallized, many of the basic values by which France lives.

1. National Independence

One value, to begin with, is a feeling for national independence. While France has sometimes carried war into other countries (notably under Louis XIV and Napoleon), the fact is that she had been more frequently invaded than invader. She has been the goal, and not the source, of migrations. Since the days of the Saracens, the invaders had been driven back, but the memory of invasion remained. The memories of oppression and plundering by foreigners, and the enormous efforts required for the liberation of the country—these have remained alive in French consciousness to this day.

Historically, the Jacobins of the French Revolution gave shape to France's concept of national independence in the famous "Committee of Public Safety." Their idea was that the security of the country rested on an armed people, and not on any military class or caste. Jacobinism, in this respect, identified aristocrats, monarchists, and ultramontane Catholics as antirepublicans and, in consequence, as traitors to France. Although this democratically based Jacobinism was later capable of transforming itself into "Caesarian," dictatorial, and antiparliamentary movements (or tolerating them) it has remained, nevertheless, a basic part of France's political tradition, to which at least lip service must be given. For the idea of national independence persists throughout the country as a fundamental value.

It must be kept in mind, however, that the unanimous homage paid to the idea of national independence, which involves also peace and security, is of a formal character. In the face of concrete divergent values (objects of action) it constitutes only an attitude. Unanimity ceases, in fact, as soon as it becomes necessary to ask what, in a given situation, constitutes true independence, or what are the means for the attainment of hic et nunc security, or by what methods a nation can preserve both peace and power.

Such questions, once posed, result in divergent reactions. One group of Frenchmen may, in the name of national independence, desire to create the mystic idea of the "mission" of universal peace; another may escape in a feeling of extreme nationalism; a third may dream of a purely French existence in complete isolation from the rest of the world, living behind supposedly impregnable barriers.

*This chapter is based mainly on Dr. Eric Weil's paper, "Myth and Faith," MS.

1

Thus we see that the French idea of national independence (and unity) does not mean unanimity, or even the recognition that those who advocate different means of achieving the desired national goal are necessarily sincere. Unanimity is prevented by the existing and widely accepted idea of treason—the latter based on the assumption that the adversary is not only an infidel but also "bought by the foreigner"—and by the religious value that is attributed to one's own "truth." (In this respect it would be interesting to analyze the influence of the Catholic ideal of a unique truth, a truth that is absolutely determinable at any moment. All French ideologies seem to be heirs to this ideal, to such an extent that he who does not adhere to it, but defends the idea of a continuous acceptance of ever limited truths, is taken, and sometimes takes himself, as a skeptic.) Contrary to the Anglo-American countries, France has, even outside of the political level, three parties, rather than two. There are two extreme parties, polarized to one another, and a central one that is opposed to the two extremes in so far as violence is concerned, but inwardly reflecting the two polar tendencies.

Unity as a defense against the invader (military, economic, ideological) may, where the danger is recognized by the citizens as imminent, bring about unity of action. The latter, however, neither produces nor demands unanimity, not even the limited unanimity of compromise. In addition, it must be said, despite its seeming contradiction, that each ideological group pretends to base unanimity on a total and true system. Hence each struggle of ideas, so long as it remains in the realm of ideas, is irreconcilable, precisely because every idea has the tendency to develop into a system of universal explanations and appreciations. Finally, we must note that the groups based on common interests are impelled in France, perhaps more so than in other countries, to justify their concrete programs by universal considerations. They are impelled to do so on account of their realization that a program has value only through the mission it serves.

2. Aims of the Individual

It is, of course, arbitrary to define the ideal of life (or even several ideals) of the members of a community. The aims of the individuals are not conceived of independently of the aims of the community even if the private ideal is opposed to that of the latter. Furthermore, no statistical data on these questions exist in France. The only available information must be based on direct observation of actuality and on a reading of history and literature. Such data must be used with caution, as a working hypothesis to be judged according to whether it does or does not succeed in making the actions and reactions of the members of the community understandable.

With these reservations in mind, we may consider the French ideal of private life as determined by two contradictory but coexistent tendencies that dominate in turn groups, individuals, and that aggregation of the latter known as the nation. These two tendencies may be designated by the concepts of happiness and salvation.

(a) <u>Happiness</u>. —For happiness, as the Frenchman understands it, neither success (material or other) nor the fulfillment of some special desire is essential. The idea of happiness has its source in the Roman concept <u>otium</u> <u>cum</u> <u>dignitate</u>— leisure with dignity— which means a form of existence recognized as valuable by those whom one considers one's equals. It may receive its contents from anywhere, from fishing as well as from the study of astronomy or from gardening or from participating in politics or from any form that involves deliberation and criticism.

What is necessary for such an existence is, in the first place, economic independence or, if that is missing, a measure of economic security, such as a retirement pension or a business that leaves some leisure. In the second place, it is necessary to have personal independence, which means no employer or master who could give orders. Third, it requires a certain amount of social importance, the latter deriving either from the esteem due to economic independence or from participation in community affairs or from membership in a respected group (churchwarden, Freemason, bowling club member, etc.).

The conditions for happiness as set forth here exclude any political action in the strict sense of the term, that is, any enterprise that demands or threatens to develop into a change of conditions. What is acceptable is political activity that does not aim at transformation but at preservation of the status quo. On the other hand, those who do not share in the material conditions required for happiness, or who consider themselves excluded from them, tend to support any political or ideological movement that would overthrow the existing system and ensure for them access to the desired life. In both instances Frenchmen, although seemingly diametrically in opposition, aim at stability: in the first group, stabilization of that which exists; in the second, the establishment of a new society in which such stabilization would become possible for themselves.

(b) <u>Salvation</u>. — The ideal of happiness is fundamentally different from the one inspired by <u>salvation</u>. While according to the former a happy life has an intrinsic value, a value all its own, the latter is characterized by the endeavor to find such a value for an existence which in itself appears to be without meaning, interest, or dignity.

This may be sought in most diverse ways. The seeker may enter a convent, join a radical party, create his own system, devote himself to poetry, or pursue adventure. What matters is to leave the beaten track, since the search for the meaning of life scorns and rejects implicitly the concept of happiness. In this way that which is discovered, or thought, to be new presents itself under the aspect of originality and implies that the values left behind are dull, stupid, insipid, and timorous.

The types described here, it should be kept in mind, are ideal— abstractions not found in reality. It would be absolutely wrong to classify Frenchmen in one or the other of the two categories. On the contrary, French individuals, groups, and the nation oscillate most of the time between the two ideals, and many contradictions of French life (not only in politics) can be explained by this fundamental ambivalence. It also explains why we find in France more tribunes than statesmen, more heroes than organizers, more poets than men of cold and calculated action. Precisely because the Frenchman inclines to extremes, he has embraced the ideal of the golden mean or correct measure—at least when he reflects. When he ponders over his values without pursuing them, he is also likely to be impressed by the boredom involved in technical organization and perseverance. This helps to explain the absence of newspapers that contain objective information. Exceptions do, of course, exist, at least in the realm of professed intentions, but ordinarily the journalist is expected to take a "religious" position. Administrative and technical details arouse boredom, and the journalist himself shares in general the preferences of his readers who do not so much wish to be informed as to see themselves edified, defended, inspired, and their beliefs justified.

In the light of all this, it is erroneous to accept the noisy discussions among intellectuals, the cry for reform, for revolt, for all aspects of the absolute, as representing the whole of French reality. In France, it should never be forgotten, those who articulate are apt to be the extremists.

The foreign observer is likely to be mistaken about the relative importance of the values of happiness and salvation in French life. As expressed by the articulate intellectuals, these values seem to come very near to shattering the nation's unity and to destroying the apparatus of the State. Actually, it is quite probable that these noisy struggles of ideas reach such an extent and vocal importance only because the nation's central organization, the government, feels itself strong enough to let those discussions have their free course. This, however, does not exclude the possibility that the members of the national administration, who by virtue of their office maintain peace and order, may declare themselves—in so far as they are individuals and free citizens—for this or that ideological side; or they may, being Frenchmen, tend to a skepticism that declares any action whatsoever to be insane.

One cannot stress too strongly the theoretical and abstract character of these two conceptions of life—happiness and salvation. These values interpenetrate the life of nearly every Frenchman, who vacillates between the two. This is true to such an extent that it is virtually impossible to decide, in any given case, whether the observer is confronted with a Frenchman who is a revolutionary trying to realize the conditions of his (or his group's) happiness, or a man who attempts to put into practice the ideal of salvation from which he cannot hope to gain any advantage for himself.

(c) Estheticism. — Another value, which does not in itself form an ideal of life, is the important role of esthetics so keenly felt by the French. This value is not one that separates Frenchmen, but it is a trait that distinguishes the French from many other nations. The esthetic value derives in great part from the otium cum dignitate kind of happiness, but the two do not necessarily coincide. The same esthetic ideal could be pursued in entirely different realms (i. e. , the ideal of the gentleman). While the Frenchman aspires alternately to happiness and salvation, he generally adheres to esthetic values. The latter are extremely rich and well developed, and although they do not influence all the strata of the population to the same degree, they do pervade the nation. The elegance and precision of expression, the correctness of speech, the respect for well-done work, the disgust for the coarse in manners as well as in occupations (that is one reason why the Frenchman does not voluntarily accept a crude and mechanical job, even if it is well paid), the love for the spiritual and artistic, the scorn for everything that is, or is considered to be, primitive— all this has long characterized the urban masses and has spread more and more even among the population of the countryside. This prevalence of esthetic values constitutes the basis of French sensibility. In France hypocrisy is less often homage paid to moral virtue than to the beautiful, the noble, and the refined.

What the foreigner calls French vanity, what strikes him as "French cultural imperialism," stems from this specific form of sensibility. A Frenchman wants to be recognized as a man of good taste, as a cultured, educated, sensitive person. He adheres to forms, and demands them of others as well as of himself. He reproves that which is not well expressed and often ends with not recognizing the inner value of a work or a person if the outside form is not beautiful. He is prone to scorn the ways of acting and living of others, particularly of foreigners, their fashions, cooking, and poetry, but he is ready at the same time to accept the work of an outsider so long as it can be appreciated within the French esthetic categories. (This is the reason why Shakespeare has fervent admirers in France, but no public.)

The esthetic attitude, although an important feature of the French character, does not directly influence the great decisions of the nation. But it does enter into the reflections of practically every individual and plays its part in his day-to-day choices.

3. The Ideals of the Community

In the preceding pages we have described the values; now we shall group them. As in the previous analyses, we do not claim here to be complete, but merely to indicate the main lines. Of these lines, we will single out two— revolutionism and traditionalism. These two lines parallel those of happiness and salvation, and, indeed, are shared by the representatives of the two schools.

(a) Revolutionism. — Revolutionism, or the revolutionary tradition, is characterized by the concepts of liberty, equality, and fraternity.

The concept of fraternity is the one that least corresponds to reality. It is usually confused with equality: human beings are brothers, hence equals. It may also be confused with liberty: since all are brothers, no one can command the other without consent.

The concept of equality (the same remarks apply also to liberty) possesses an incomparably greater strength, since it admits criticism of existing conditions. Nothing seems to be easier than to find a precise meaning for "equality" than by pointing out the existing inequalities. Originally, "equality" meant equality before the law of all citizens. In the nineteenth century, the growth of anarchistic, socialist, and communist ideas has transferred the concept of equality from the judicial and constitutional to the economic level. The redistribution of property and the equalization of income were part of all programs devised in the revolutionary tradition; they have inspired domestic French politics since the beginning of this century. Their influence has been great. Such reforms as progressive taxation, sickness and old-age insurance, nationalization of certain basic private enterprises (see Chapter IV this book, pp. 45–60), and others derived from this revolutionary tradition. In addition, free public instruction (adopted for secondary schools on the eve of the second World War) was intended to give future citizens equality of education. The introduction of the system of competition for every office of any importance in the national administration, as well as for admission to every great school, was intended to protect the equality of opportunity for all.

Up to recent years the tendency was not so much toward equality of opportunity as toward equalitarianism. It seemed important to level down rather than up. More recently the problem of raising the general level has become obvious, and it seems to be understood that the equality of the citizens is justified only if it produces an aristocracy of efficiency by encouraging the individual efforts through material and psychological compensations, by surrounding deserved success with a halo, by protecting both the specialists and the generally qualified individuals from a too sharp lowering of their standard of living. This general change has been favored by the fact that the main party of the social revolution gave up, under the influence of the Russian example, equalitarianism in favor of an open aristocracy of talents. Nevertheless, it is probably still too early to speak of the disappearance of equalitarianism in France.

(b) Traditionalism. — French traditionalism is a product of the Revolution of 1789. Its main values (difficult to summarize, since we do not have here an official doctrine, but only a multitude of sects and schools) are centered around the concepts of order, morals, and authority.

Traditionalism, although from its beginnings monarchistic by conviction, was quick to acquire a republican and democratic language. Since the end of the nineteenth century the Royalists as such have not had any influence in France. But the traditionalists preserve the ideals of a paternal (not fraternal), authoritarian (not free), hierarchic (not equalitarian) State.

The attraction of the traditionalist arguments consists in the nostalgic memory of France's ancient grandeur, which is unfavorably compared with the faults and weaknesses of the Republic, and the latter's scandals, disorders, lack of initiative. Since the weaknesses are clear and known to all, they make a strong impression, while the identical or corresponding faults of the past are either unknown or conveniently forgotten.

One observes in France periodical crises of "Caesarism" or "Bona-partism," movements that pretend to reconcile the revolutionary, particularly the Jacobin, tradition with the traditionalist one. Such movements promise freedom, but under the surveillance of an enlightened government, the only one qualified to understand the interests of the nation. They also promise equality, but with the qualification that only the "good" citizens participate in the management of public affairs. Caesarism or Bonapartism (or Pétainism, for that matter) offers the citizen social progress, but only under the condition that he remain within the sphere of his individual activity. It should be noted that all movements of this type in recent times have found support among Catholics. On the other hand, these movements may profit from the Jacobin tradition when the patrie is "in danger" or "betrayed."

These traditional values remain strongest in private life. The coherence of the family remains as firm as ever. Private morals, as opposed to public ones, are relatively high. (It is permissible to cheat the "rich" and the "exploiter" but not the "poor" and "unfortunate.") Christian tradition is alive, although in many circles it has shed all doctrinal and ritualistic character and presents itself as humanitarian, vaguely Kantian ethics or ethics of enlightened self-interest. Established institutions— university, magistracy, administration, army— continue to enjoy traditional respect. Thus, the values that have suffered defeat on the political level maintain a strong influence on the social-personal level, despite the fact that efforts of the political traditionalists to monopolize these values make the latter sometimes appear as screens for antidemocratic activities.

4. The Relation Between the Values in the Last Half-Century

The modern development of Traditionalism and Revolutionism dates from the Dreyfus affair and the reconciliation between the Vatican and the French Republic. These two events practically wiped out the older monarchistic and Catholic-clerical traditionalism.

Traditionalism, which until that period had been opposed to social reforms, elaborated its own social doctrine and started to make alliances with movements which had similar goals. Revolutionism, on the other hand, under the pressure of labor unions and their sympathizers, gradually shifted from the juridical to the social sphere of activities. At the same time the army, whose chiefs had been discredited by the Dreyfus affair, was more and more subjected to parliamentary control and began to accept the principle of social and educational responsibility. The old clerical-Royalist alliance of "saber and aspergillum" was to a large extent broken.

Since then the idea of social justice has figured in the program of every French group. There is unanimity about a whole series of goals to be attained. Among the latter are: minimum income, social insurance, old-age pensions, family allowances, birth premiums, free education in the lower and middle grades, scholarships for the poor, admission to all careers regardless of social origin.

Thus, a great change took place both among the traditionalist, Catholic

circles, which now accepted the idea of social reform, and among the
liberals of the revolutionary tradition who likewise came to support the
Welfare State. However, this agreement as to ends does not extend to means.
In regard to the latter, opinions are still divided as to how best to achieve
social justice.

The two extreme groups— Traditionalists and Revolutionists— teach
that only an absolute authority is able to achieve the desired social goals.
The Center maintains that only through free discussion of problems and
methods can the goal be attained. One of the extremes, the Traditionalist,
bases its ideal upon the value of the human personality as understood from
the standpoint of Christian transcendentalism (equality of the immortal
soul) and demands a hierarchic society. The other extreme, the Revolutionist, is convinced that the true revolution still remains to be carried
out; it justifies its position with a philosophy of history which claims to
show that the march toward a society without private property and without
classes is inevitable. The Center, inclining either to one or to the other
side but rejecting dictatorship as well as revolution, tries to soothe dis-
satisfactions, but is careful not to tie itself too closely to any particular
method. Its efforts are motivated mainly by a dread of internal violence.

The same unanimity concerning ends but disagreement concerning means
exists also in foreign affairs. Here sympathies are determined by and reflect domestic politics. Thus Traditionalists and Centrists favor the United
States and Revolutionists support the Soviet Union. The conceptions of the
kind of peace that is desirable also vary. Traditionalists hope for the realization of universal peace— which is desired by all— through agreements
among the existing governments. Revolutionists argue that global peace
can be brought about only by mass movements and the intervention of "the
country of the revolution" through a number of stages, such as a war of
liberation, social revolution, and a dictatorship for the suppression of the
State.

Here an important development is to be noted. Certain ideological conflicts which, in the past, had seemed irreconcilable have now been seriously
weakened. Traditionalism's exasperated militarism of pre-World War I
currently has no more adherents than the corresponding radical antimilitarism. Anarchistic antistatism is maintained only in a few limited intellectual circles; the same is true of that traditionalism which has always
opposed social change. Individualism has abandoned its social atomism to
the same extent as collectivism has given recognition to the existence of
personality. Nationalism has recognized the necessity of a regulated international life, and internationalism refers to the values of the country's
traditions.

This development has accelerated through World War II and is moving
toward an increasing agreement as far as values are concerned. But the
extent of that agreement is far from unanimous. On the strictly ideological
level two strategic principles confront one another: (1) the liberation of the
individual as the first step toward internal and universal peace with equality

of rights and duties, and (2) the establishment of internal and global peace through a dictatorial revolution with a view to the final liberation of the individual.

Thus the struggle between the different schools of thought goes on. However, it is less a conflict of opposing ideas than a struggle for the right legitimately to represent those ideas.

The invocation of the same ideals by all parties tends to rob them of a good deal of their emotional value. Actually, what determines final decisions is France's international position; questions that until recently seemed purely domestic are nowadays decided on the basis of confidence or distrust of the two world powers. Former opposing concepts ("reason vs. faith," "parliamentary democracy vs. traditional authority," "revolution vs. order," "individualism vs. collectivism," "pacifism vs. militarism," "universalism vs. traditionalism") have become blurred. New theories for the formulation and concepts and the crystallization of preferences have not yet been worked out. Current movements and ideas— atheistic existentialism, Christian personalism, social capitalism, liberal socialism, Communist humanism, pacifist nationalism— show a tendency to resolve the problem of "individual vs. society" rather than a concrete formulation for the practical guidance of adherents. This weakness, however, seems to be shared by all modern societies, and not by France alone.

5. Classes and Ideologies

As we have seen, until about the end of the nineteenth century humanitarian and international ideals belonged to the domain of the revolutionary heritage, while the ideals of order and legitimacy were the preserve of the traditionalists. This cleavage was reflected also in the class divisions. On the one side were aligned the workers, the lower strata of the bourgeoisie, and a large number of intellectuals; on the other side were the great bourgeoisie, including many of the "respectable" little bourgeois, and the rural estate owners. The former were freethinkers, deists, nonconformists generally; the latter were Catholic-clerical.

In recent decades, however, these dividing lines have become somewhat blurred. Nowadays it is possible to find all ideologies in all the classes. One part of the "capitalist" bourgeoisie has gone over to the "proletarian" side, one part of the proletariat has found its way back to the Church. On the other hand, there has been a tendency toward the strengthening of class loyalty in the face of weakened national organizations or elites. The parliamentary scandals, for example, resulted in the discrediting of many men whose influence had once been great.

Class interests continue to play an important role in the political, intellectual, and moral life of the nation. The group which we have described as the Center recruits itself mainly from the contented or rising strata— peasants, bourgeoisie, high officials. Leftist extremism, representing about one-fourth of the voting population, finds its adherents among a large section of the proletariat. The majority of the petty and middle officeholders are more evolutionist than revolutionist. Employees and handicraftsmen vacillate between revolution and evolution. Caesarian extremism is to be found in those circles that are afraid of losing status and privilege, in those who have suffered a comedown and who see themselves robbed of their position by the social and political evolution, among those who dread any kind of disorder— in short, by the great bourgeoisie, the impoverished petty bourgeoisie, and the public agents of authority as well as the farmers.

These divisions are not, however, always rigid. One may find workmen who are Catholic, miners who oppose secular schools, and members of the middle class who are inspired by a spirit of social justice. There are even priests who, on the social level, take a position favorable to revolutionary and dictatorial doctrines which treat religion as a survival from primitive times and as an opium of the people.

6. The Conflicts of Loyalty

Something needs to be said about the social position and function of the intellectuals. They are often economically independent, as professors, rentiers, journalists with fixed positions, officeholders, or employees. Almost without exception they live in Paris, forming a center apart from the rest of the city, and maintaining close personal relations. Detached from the traditional structures as well as from the classes, they are extremely influential without taking any definite responsibility. It is rare for them to enter practical politics or take a high post in the national administration. French intellectuals have no experience in practical affairs and are inclined more to metaphysical than to concrete questions. They leave the latter to the "specialists," for whom they have little regard.

In the writings of the intellectuals one detects, in particular, conflicts of loyalty. In general, two different kinds of loyalty are now discernible: (1) to attitudes and (2) to institutions. In the first case, values do not come into question and are not analyzed. Only preferences are stated and labeled. Thus one belongs to the left, or one is for or against the bourgeois way of life, or one is for the oppressed or for the poor, or for order and discipline, or for faith. In the second case, the preferences derive from class identifications. Thus a peasant will make his decision as a peasant, and a workman as a proletarian. This is especially true in the case of organizations that are strongly hierarchic and claim universality, notably the Catholic Church and the Communist Party. Adherents of these two groups find their loyalties defined by universal criteria.

In sum, concrete decisions and loyalties often depend on organizations rather than ideologies. For a long time the Catholic Church has been the only institution with a "total" doctrine. It has withdrawn from actual political and social strife and merely reserves for itself the right to condemn actions, organizations, or individuals of which it disapproves. It preaches its ideals without taking sides in the political arena, wishing, in so far as possible, its faithful to avoid any conflict of conscience that might decide against the Church. Now there is on the scene a kind of rival, the Communist Party, organized as a church after the pattern of the Roman Catholic and possessing, in the eyes of its adherents, an authority qualified to decide all questions which hitherto had been the preserve of the Roman Church.

The appearance of the Communist Party has wrought a change in the French scene on the political and other levels. In the past, Catholicism has had its roots in a foreign country, but only on the spiritual level. Now, for the first time in French history, the source of an important movement that arouses loyalties is not only situated abroad, but is also tied up with a nonspiritual, political-military foreign power of the first magnitude. For the French Communists this does not result in a conflict of loyalties between their adherence to the Soviet Union and their love of France. They believe they serve the true interests of France by serving those of the world revolution. But a true conflict does arise for those who are ready to accept the aims of the proletarian revolution but who do not think that the policy of that revolution, as it is carried out by the Soviet Union, serves the interests of France as they perceive them.

We have here another instance, mentioned before, of the influence of foreign politics on domestic affairs. The reaction to communism has been a rapprochement between the "Caesarian" tendencies and those of the Center, for both are convinced that the values of the French tradition must be defended against the "foreign" menace—an argument used in retaliation also by the Communists. It should be noted, however, that here, too, the question is more one of attitude than of basic values, since both parties maintain, probably in equally good faith, that they believe in the same aims and that the adversary is the one who betrays what he pretends to worship.

But all these conflicts, in so far as they are conflicts of values, are the expressions of only a handful of individuals. Nowhere in the world do we find large numbers of people asking themselves whether their decisions derive from coherent principles. In this France is no exception. In France, where attitudes are firmly rooted, leaders of the parties are rarely asked to explain their philosophical and moral system; the latter are simply taken for granted. What is expected from the leaders is that they will not betray one's "ideal." The latter is an affective preference that seeks some concrete expression. "Negative" values—clericalism, anticlericalism, internationalism, revolution, disorder, dictatorship, personal regime, atheism (which are negative for their opponents only)—play a great role, because it is easier to determine what one does not like than to define in any given situation what one does like.

This in no way contradicts what was said before, namely, that the values of peace, international collaboration, human dignity along with security and mutual respect, are common to almost the entire nation. An appeal to these ideals is not only sure of universal approval, but might also evoke a determined readiness for national and personal sacrifice.

II. THE IDEA OF DEMOCRACY AND THE POLITICAL INSTITUTIONS*

The French idea of democracy cannot be understood without recourse to history. "Traces of former regimes," said André Siegfried, "exist throughout our conception of government; their analysis requires retrospective presentation."[1] And, more recently, David Thomson, in his Democracy in France, stated that "the study of the Third Republic cannot be separated from a consideration of the entire development of modern France."[2]

A. The Traditional Idea of Democracy

1. Persistence of Opposition to Democracy

The first fact that needs to be emphasized is that democracy has never met with unanimous acceptance in France. From the Revolution of 1789 to our day it has always had opponents who have contested the validity of its basic principles and have not despaired of its overthrow.

Established in 1875 by the National Assembly with a majority of only one vote, the Third Republic had to repulse constantly the assault of the reactionary forces which were attempting its destruction because they detested its principles. The Boulangists in 1887—89, the Dreyfus affair in 1898—1900, the agitation of the antiparliamentarian leagues after February 6, 1934— these have been the most visible symptoms of this unceasing hostility to the Republic. In 1940, owing to the military defeat,† antidemocratic elements seized power; the "French State" of Vichy, which effaced even the name of the Republic from postage stamps and coins, sanctioned their triumph, which was fortunately temporary. Many political forces, apparently devoted to democracy for years, threw off their masks and joined the Vichyites.

Why this persistence of a current of thought and political action hostile to democracy?

At the roots of the opposition to democracy there is indisputably a matter of principle; a conviction that no society can endure except under a hierarchy, and that the people, the masses, are "incapable of governing themselves or of governing others."[3] A pessimistic idea of human nature— an idea of Catholic origin, and directly opposed to the optimism of J. J. Rousseau— is at the basis of this conviction; man, being naturally evil, must have teachers, or guides, to direct him toward good. These guides are the traditional institutions, the social authorities. The first is the authority of monarchy, temporally the highest, and then the First Families, predestined by birth and wealth to a leading role. Finally, above all, there is the Catholic Church, charged with shaping conscience and soul and conditioning them toward the social order and eternal salvation. To those who believe in the

---

*By Francois Goguel.
†See Chapter V, Section 1.

12

divine origin of monarchical power, the Revolution of 1789 appeared to be a sacrilege, and the fatal consequences which they attributed to it seemed to be God's punishment of a rebellious nation. These theocratic ideas, expounded by Bonald at the time of the Restoration, survived much longer than one would have believed possible; at the time of the defeat of 1940 we personally heard them expressed by an army chaplain, to the great dismay of most of his listeners, even good Catholics.

The fact that, in France, during the Revolution of 1789 as well as later, the partisans of democracy had been for the most part the adversaries of Catholicism, and the fact that they had always wanted to free the citizens politically as well as intellectually from obscurantism, led the Church of France to side with the adversaries of democracy. By an inevitable reaction, this antidemocratic attitude of the Church has contributed largely to making the democrats its implacable enemies. A search for the initial responsibilities would be of but little interest here. The essential point is to establish that, until the first World War, the Church, as a body, despite some individual exceptions, whether priests or laymen, has appeared irrevocably hostile to democracy. "No militant Leftist," wrote André Siegfried in 1930, "has yet been able to believe that the Church can sincerely work for the Republic."[4]

These, then, are primarily the theoretical doctrines and, strictly speaking, the religious principles which are found at the heart of the persistent opposition to democracy in France.

Business interests also have their place in this opposition. First during the Revolution, then throughout the nineteenth century—and even before there was any question of socialism—all attempts to install democracy manifested themselves in a violent form. The revolutionary uprisings, riots, and barricades in Lyons and Paris which occurred during the July Monarchy and the Second Republic terrified the middle classes. They understood quickly enough that the claim to political equality would necessarily entail a claim to social equality, and that a democracy in power could not disassociate itself from the material lot of the lower classes. Thus is explained the fact that the French middle class, after revolting against the ancien régime and its nobility in 1789, allied itself more and more in the course of the nineteenth century to either the avowed or the clandestine adversaries of democracy.

Finally, a certain number of Frenchmen joined the adversaries of democracy for less selfish reasons, mainly because it seemed to them to be inefficient and unproductive. In fact, we shall see that democracy in its traditional concept, which predominated in France during a good part of the Third Republic, was more of an organization of resistance to power than a method of government. Among those who believed that State power was necessary there was a progressive alienation which amounted to a veritable hostility to democracy. "The Republic," said Charles Seignobos, "appears to have been established by the idealism of Paris, by the serious-minded elements of the East and by the turbulent elements of the South."[5]

It is significant to note that the provinces of the east, which until 1898 always gave a majority to the candidates of the democratic Left in the elections, have regularly voted for the Right since the Dreyfus affair; this was because the Left became hostile to the army.

The form of democracy, if not its principles, has thus for half a century provoked the hostility of certain categories of the French population, which it is possible to locate geographically. What is known of the psychology of the French of the east as compared to that of the French of the south allows us to believe that it was by its disdain of efficiency and of sincerity in its methods of government that the Republic has progressively alienated many of those who had originally contributed to its foundation.

2. The Traditional Concept of Democracy

We have just said that on the whole the traditional concept of democracy in France is less a conception of government than a conception of the resistance of the citizen to power— including that of the State.

David Thomson explains, "It became usual to consider democracy and government as two distinct poles of political life, too distant from each other for the vital spark of democratic government to be able to flash between them."[6] The part played by "reasons of State" and by "necessities of government" in the arguments invoked by the conservatives against the partisans of democratic reform— either of a political or social nature— has certainly contributed in a decisive way to anchoring in the minds of the latter the idea of an essential antinomy between democracy and government. In 1923–24, when the Radical newspaper Le Quotidien campaigned against the parties of the Right, which were then in power, its masthead affirmed that this paper was "the defender of the governed"— a slogan that was not abandoned even when a ministry of the Left was set up. In the minds of the suspicious French provincials, every government and the men who compose it, no matter how sincerely democratic they may have been in the beginning, become suspect.

The essential aim sought by the partisans of democracy is not so much the conquest of power as the formation of a Leftist opposition sufficiently powerful to counterbalance the government (which is necessarily reactionary) and to prevent it from doing anything. Such a state of mind is not only true of intellectuals. It is found, barely modified, among the lower classes, principally in the departments of the south of France where there is a great social stability— the stability of a class of peasant landowners, often well to do— and it is accompanied by an ineradicable faithfulness to the political opinions of the extreme Left. This explains the thought of a Communist mayor of a commune in the Drome, who declared that he and his friends were apprehensive of seeing their party become too powerful "because it would then run the risk of taking over power." Those who voted for Communist candidates did not want power, but only wished to strengthen the opposition party in order to enable it to act as an efficient counterweight to the government. It goes without saying that such a conception implies a great indifference to the action of State power. There is not only a profound skepticism about the usefulness or necessity of the measures taken by the government to guard the general interests of the country in a conservative way, but there is also a nearly total indifference toward concrete reforms. "The true power of the electors . . . is defined, I believe, more by resistance to the authorities than by reform action. "[7]

We have here a state of mind truly characteristic of an individualistic and stable society, which survives today in a good half of the departments of France. Economically such a society is formed by a large number of small production units— agricultural or artisan— parallel but not interdependent. The fate of these enterprises depends much more on the individual qualities of those who direct them than on the action of the State. As for those whom birth has not made economically independent, it seems that by work and economy— again individual qualities— they can become so, provided that they are given sufficient education. Hence the importance of the school problem in the eyes of the militant politicians of those regions, not only as a means of struggling against the obscurantist influence of the Catholic Church, but also as an essential instrument for the realization of social justice. In fact, social justice, in an economic society which is so simple and, so to speak, precapitalist, does not seem to depend so much on a reform of the distribution of property and wages as on an equality of opportunity, given from the beginning to every individual, thanks to equal education for all.

Considering this state of affairs Robert de Jouvenel wrote in 1914, "France is a happy land where the soil is divided. Politics there is a matter of individual taste, not a condition of life. "[8]

Thus is explained an indifference to social productivity and economic progress which most informed observers agree in recognizing as a fundamental element in the traditional idea of political democracy in France. What counts above all else are principles, doctrines. Ideas come before realities because they are laden with a symbolical value. "I am willing, " Alain said, "for the rich to exist and to wear out the roads in their automobiles, but I am not willing to have them call themselves masters . . . and finally, since inequality is everywhere, I want equality to be loudly affirmed. "[9]

These principles are primarily those concerning the position of the individual in society. The great claim of the traditional French democratic spirit in this regard is equality rather than liberty. This spirit was formed in a society in which liberty was not seriously threatened, but in which equality clashed with the vestiges of the ancien régime and the claims of the "social authorities" to monopolize the controlling role. When Gambetta defined the Republic as "the advent of new social strata" it was against this claim of the nobility and the upper bourgeoisie that he was protesting. It was not a matter of modifying the economic structure of traditional French society, which did not seem to permit an unbearable inequality in material conditions, but of changing its political structure, which was essentially a matter of introducing new principles into the customs of the nation.

Although French democracy may be indifferent to great material enterprises and even to positive social reforms, it is not limited solely to abstractions. For, even in a society of independent workmen and farmers, most of whose members possess the economic basis of real individual independence, the political domination of an aristocracy of notables constitutes an undeniable reality which can transmit itself into daily life by means of a multitude of incidents, trivial in appearance, but profoundly significant.

But this individualistic democracy is also too often a short-sighted one. The inveterate distrust it feels toward "the necessities of government," the personal conviction that the government is useless, that in any case the proper duties incumbent upon it are limited to the maintenance of a certain order and to the diffusion of education— all those psychological traits, which are characteristic of a peasant society without broad contacts with the world, become singularly dangerous when they determine the policies of a great power involved in the course of modern industrialization and urbanization.

But it is not only on the Right that traditional French democracy has provoked opposition by its inefficient nature and its indifference to ideas of productivity and efficiency. The Left also became critical of it.

3. Social Democracy and Popular Democracy

Socialism, up to the war of 1914, gained adherents not because it rejected democracy but as a necessary development of it. Socialists did not regard democracy as erroneous but as incomplete. They felt that social democracy must be joined to political democracy in order to give it its full meaning.

In large towns and among the salaried workers of modern industry it was impossible to continue thinking that diffusion of education would be sufficient to equalize the opportunities of everyone from the outset. Diversity of individual qualities no longer was able to account for inequality of conditions. Work and economy no longer offered a guaranty of economic independence. Thus, in so far as aspirations toward liberty were related to a thirst for equality, it seemed that it was the very structure of the economic system which constituted an invincible obstacle. Hence there arose a demand for a transformation of this system, first, for the sake of creating social institutions fitted to guarantee security and dignity in the life of ownership from anonymous shareholders to the men who were directly engaged in the means of production. For such was really the meaning of the term "social democracy"; it meant an economic system in which the control of industry would no longer belong to capital but to labor, no longer to an oligarchy of money but to the masses, just as political democracy had transferred sovereignty, at least theoretically, from the notables to the whole nation.

The champions of social democracy could not share the indifference of the traditional democrats toward reform. Nor could they share their individualistic philosophy. Ideas of social productivity and efficiency being familiar to the social democrats, they did not shrink from the prospect of the collective disciplines which were indispensable to the success of great material enterprises. Yet these objectives did not seem to them to be incompatible with the maintenance of the political institutions of a classical democracy entailing plurality of parties, freedom of elections, permanent control of the executive power by a sovereign assembly, and the independence of the judiciary. At the most they envisaged some alterations of this mechanism, in order to organize democracy better, thanks to proportionate representation (which was ardently demanded by the Socialists before 1914) and to the action of mass political parties.

But after the first World War it was no longer a question of extending political democracy into social democracy. Differing from their socialist predecessors, the Communists vigorously contested the value of the traditional institutions. Putting sole emphasis on the economic and social factors of political power, they declared that the right to vote did not really give the economically weak groups any way of protecting their interests or of participating effectively in the control of public affairs. On the contrary, according to them, the heads of the powerful industrial and financial interests, which had appeared with the development of capitalism, had at their disposal, by the very fact of their economic power, the means of irresistible pressure on the State. Hence the desire of the Communists to destroy by force that State which seemed to them more capitalistic than democratic, and to install by revolutionary means a "dictatorship of the proletariat," which would basically assure the defense of the interest of the masses and the emancipation of the proletariat. In short, in order to realize the traditional aims of democracy— equality and liberty— which they conceived exclusively in economic terms, the Communists proposed to discard the methods of political democracy. In a system of plurality of parties, elections seemed to them not as good a way of expressing the real will of the masses as to the action of a popular party, embodying that will.

This concept, which we shall call "popular democracy," is seen to be completely opposed both to the traditional idea of political democracy and to the more elaborated idea of social democracy. The Communists' regard for efficiency and revolutionary action, which found expression in their idea of an at least transitory dictatorship of the proletariat, answered some of the aspirations of the supporters of social democracy who were disheartened by the purely ideological and symbolical aspects of the traditional political democracy. The very idea of an authoritarian and omnipotent democratic State— today we call it totalitarian— is deeply rooted in the Jacobin tradition of the great Revolution. In other respects, by the very fact that the Communists constituted an opposition party, oriented further to the Left than any of the others, they were almost automatically destined to get the support of the many voters, mostly from the Midi, for whom the final aim of political action consisted of paralyzing the government, which they conceived to be by nature reactionary. Finally, industrial development, accelerated by the first World War, increased the proletarian type of social groups, which were predisposed by their often precarious material condition to listen favorably to the propaganda of a party which saw in the proletariat a necessary instrument of historical evolution and the legitimate heir of the former controlling classes.

4. The Crisis of the Traditional Idea of Democracy

The Third Republic found itself, at the outbreak of the second World War, exposed to attacks from both the Right and the Left of the partisans of popular democracy. On the Right the progressive industrialization of France had assured to the doctrinary partisans of the hierarchical and aristocratic society the co-operation of those who felt the necessity of a competent and efficient government. On the extreme Left there was the rapid increase of partisans of popular democracy, followers of the idea of the dictatorship of the proletariat and of economic and social revolution. The French democracy survived only because there existed an important segment of peasants and artisans with their individualistic and ideological concept of democracy. But this group was on the decrease during the last years of the Third Republic.

5. Economic Causes

The ideological and individualistic idea of democracy was suitable to the aspirations held in areas where the traditional small-scale economy prevailed. Today the traditional economy still covers about half of the area of France. But there are not more than two out of five Frenchmen living in a society favorable to individualism. Changes do occur, however. General economic fluctuations have repercussions in the areas of traditional economy. In a period of prosperity the modern segment of the economy draws man power from the traditional one; in a period of crisis it pays less for its products, particularly agricultural ones. By the threat of buying abroad the foodstuffs which they need, the zones of modern economy exert a slow but continuous pressure for technical progress on the others. Only by means of co-operatives can the latter progress to the benefit of small independent units of production. Indeed, there is a growth of co-operatives in peasant and artisan regions; they take the form of mutual agricultural credit, of syndicates for electrification, of co-operatives for the utilization of mechanized agricultural equipment, exchanges for the purchase of fertilizer or, in the case of the working artisan and the retail tradesman, raw materials and finished products. Thus, in the very regions in which the individualistic and ideological concept of democracy was born and where its principal base remains, ideas of collective discipline, organization, and productivity are being gradually introduced and raise fewer objections there today than they once did.

But it is in the areas of modern economy that the necessity for collective

discipline is most distinctly felt. Undoubtedly the reflexes of the fundamental individualism of the French temperament are far from having entirely disappeared there. But even there, where this instinctive individualism survives, practical necessities impose an awareness of the need
for discipline and collective action. Specialization of industries, financially
independent of each other, creates a technical interdependence between
them. The national market is dependent on the market abroad for supply
as well as for outlet. Private industries need—for example, in regard
to power and transportation—collective equipment, which can only be
provided by the State. Budgetary politics, from the point of view of public
investments as well as from that of monetary repercussions of the methods
for securing financial facilities, exercise a direct action on the activity of
the industries. The effectiveness of State action, the competency, and the
responsibility with which it accomplishes the tasks that are incumbent
upon it—which are much more complex than in the areas of traditional
economy—thus become fundamental elements in political decisions.
　　The areas of the modern economy meet more vast and acute social
problems than the areas of the traditional economy. In them the creation
of public institutions for social security is made necessary by the great
need of a laboring class population threatened with unemployment by economic fluctuations. The gravity of eventual conflicts between social classes
obliges the State to do its utmost to prevent them or to end them by compulsory arbitration.
　　Thus everything combines to make the populations in areas of the modern
economy aware of the necessity of action by political power. This helps
to undermine the traditional idea of democracy as resistance by citizens
to State power. All demand that the State act, and act effectively. It is
thus that the industrialization which France has attained since the middle
of the nineteenth century became the principal factor in the transformation
of the French individualistic idea of democracy.

6. Political Aspects

　　The defeat of 1940,* succeeding the prolongation of the world economic
crisis of the 'thirties, revealed glaringly the weakness of the traditional
democratic State and its unfitness to fulfill its fundamental duties. The
success of elements hostile to democracy at the time of the defeat of 1940,
and the strong support that the government of Vichy received among classes
which had hitherto supported the democratic Republic, constitute important
political phenomena. Vichyism reawakened the combative spirit of the militants of the Left and their distrust of everything that was related to the
conservative tradition. But it also helped to make some Leftists understand
the danger to democracy itself from a conception of the republican State
which was too purely ideological and careless of efficacy.
　　In addition, collaboration with the enemy by the most decided antidemo-

---

*See Chapter V, Section 1.

crats, and particularly those who had been touched by Fascism, undoubtedly
served the cause of democracy by discrediting in the public mind, at
least temporarily, its adversaries.

Perhaps this consideration played its part in attracting the Catholic
Church to democracy— the most striking political change which has occurred in France since World War II. Between 1919 and 1939, to be sure,
the relations between the Church and the Third Republic had considerably
improved, but not enough to disarm the traditional distrust of the militants
of the Left toward Catholicism, nor to alienate the Church from the cause
of the conservative parties. During the first years of the Vichy government
a part of the French episcopate took up cudgels for the "French State"
and Pétain, but even then the Church took a firm stand against Vichy's
anti-Semitic legislation. The presence in the ranks of the Resistance of
a considerable number of Catholics, priests and laymen, the contacts
which were established between them and the most anticlerical militants
of the Leftist parties, constituted a ferment capable of dissolving previous
distrust and hostility. Under the influence of the Catholics— whether
thinkers or men of action, prelates or mere laymen— contact was re-estab-
lished with the proletariat, which the Church had lost in the course of the
nineteenth century. The Catholic Church of France came to realize, in
the course of the second World War, the profound community of interests
of Christianity and democracy. Conforming to the attitude of the Vatican,
the Church everywhere (with the exception of that of Spain and Portugal)
openly allied itself to democracy. The Church's acceptance of democracy,
it must be pointed out, did not imply a renunciation of certain strictly
Catholic conceptions of society and the State. The latter, it should not be
forgotten, are difficult to reconcile with those of secular democracy, which
are more or less impregnated with the tradition of Rousseau and the Jacobins.

The Catholics have a naturalistic conception of society. They see in
it the combination of a large number of secondary natural societies—
churches, families, parishes, trades, universities, et cetera— each having its particular competence. To Catholics the State exercises only the
functions necessary to the life of society. In the eyes of the Catholics,
society constitutes a natural gift, which the State cannot pretend to remodel
according to a preconceived system without surpassing its rights. Nothing
is more contradictory to the Catholic conception of society and the State
than the one the Jacobins inherited from Jean Jacques Rousseau. The "intermediary bodies," that is to say, the natural communities whose existence and function are considered fundamental by the Catholics, have been
fiercely attacked by French revolutionists. French Jacobins recognize no
intermediary between citizens and the State; they consider the State as
all-powerful, and recognize in it the right, if it expresses the will of a
majority of the people, to reconstruct in its own way the order of society
as a whole. The conception of fundamental political liberties is thus rather
different among democrats of Catholic tradition from those of secular tra-

dition. Catholics stress above all the liberties of the natural groups, for example, the right of a father to give his children the kind of education he chooses. Jacobins think primarily of the liberty of the individual and admit that only the State may assume the arbitrary direction of the education of its citizens, specifically in order to free them from the hold of family or religious traditions. In the social and economic field in particular, the divergence between the fundamental Catholic conceptions of society and those of secular groups often lead to irreconcilable policies in practice.

The example of the satellite states of the Soviet Union, particularly that of the most western of these states, Czechoslovakia, made many French democrats realize the enormous importance of purely political liberties which France had attained in the course of the nineteenth century. The example of enslaved Eastern Europe led many partisans of social democracy to remember that political democracy, with the institutions which are traditionally theirs in the West, do not deserve the less to be preserved and defined. The liberty of the press, the plurality of political parties, the existence of a political opposition, the integrity of elections, the protection of citizens from arbitrary policies, regulation, the independence of the judiciary— all these fundamental characteristics of liberal regimes have certainly regained a greater value in the eyes of the French of the Left since they have seen them disappear in the states in the Soviet orbit. Although deeply concerned with equality, French democracy is nowadays more conscious of the value of liberty since it has disappeared in many parts of Europe.

These are, then, the essential aspects of the problem of adaptation of the idea of democracy in France today— a desire for efficiency and competence in the State, a necessity of making a reconciliation with the Christian democrats, a desire to preserve institutions of political liberalism, and at the same time to continue the struggle for the realization of social democracy, that is to say, the effort to assure every man a share in the profit and direction of the enterprise in which he works. Some of these aims may appear contradictory. But it is conceivable that in practice it will be possible to make a sound compromise which will give everyone his necessary place.

7. Current Trends in Search of a Solution

The concern for efficiency and competence in the State is not the monopoly of any one political party or political trend, but it is especially important in the political movement known as the Rally of the French People, created and directed by General de Gaulle. Neo-Gaullism[10] claims to be, and certainly wishes to be, democratic. But it considers it essential not to place the State entirely in the hands of the Parliament. While it accepts the principles of ministerial responsibility, freedom of elections, and the existence of political parties, it believes it necessary to entrust the functions of President of the Republic to a person elected, if not directly by universal suffrage, at least by an electoral college much larger than the Parliament and which would include the delegates of the municipal councils of the communes and the general councils of the departments.

Gaullism wants the President to represent the unity of the nation, beyond the division of parties and, when necessary, solve conflicts between Parliament and the government by dissolution of Parliament. In this way it aims to give life and strength to the republican State, to accomplish a profound reform of the administration, and to modernize the public power.

But such a program in France comes up against an obstacle which is difficult to overcome: The concept of a democratic presidential State has against it the memory of Bonapartism and the coups d'état with which Napoleon I and particularly Napoleon III ended the First and Second republics in order to establish their personal power. Such historical recollections exert a powerful action on the political sensibilities of French citizens, particularly in the country and in small towns. The place held by the personality of General de Gaulle in the political movement which he directs also disturbs those who think that "the Republic ought to distrust individuals" and who remember the use of the national prestige that Pétain made against democracy in 1940.

The Gaullists have made political blunders which have set against them the traditional forces of the Left, particularly the Socialists. Unfortunately for its aims, Gaullism has attracted the sometimes enthusiastic help of the most inveterate reactionary groups and of most of those suspected of being adversaries of the principle of democracy. Hence it seems unlikely that the Gaullists will be given a chance to develop a new conception of democracy which would be able to resolve the present crisis in France.

A certain number of political forces, heirs to the early radicalism and to the moderate parties of the Third Republic, have devoted themselves since 1947 to restoring the liberal institutions of the Third Republic. It does not seem likely that such an effort can succeed. This movement is dependent geographically and socially on the regions and classes the least affected by modern economic evolution.

More "to the Right" (but sometimes allied with the radicals and the moderates against the hazards of a neo-Gaullist or Communist venture) are the M.R.P. and the Socialist Party. Many things separate them, principally the Catholic inspiration of the former and the secular tradition of the latter. But they have in common a concern for social democracy and devotion to political democracy. [11]

Everything considered, it seems that the solution of the problem posed by the crisis of adaptation of the concept of democracy in France will depend, to a great extent, on the ability of the M.R.P. and the Socialists to apply a program of reform to the Constitution of the Fourth Republic, taking into account the experience of the past.

B. Democratic Institutions and Their Operations

1. Institutions of Political Democracy

In view of what we have said about the conceptions of democracy which predominated during the Third Republic, it is not surprising that the essential defect of the institutions of the Third Republic was the absence of effective and well-organized power.

The administration was then in a definitely subordinate position in relation to the Parliament, and especially to the Chamber of Deputies, which was elected by universal suffrage. It did not have the right of dissolution, despite the provisions contained in the Constitution to that effect. Ministerial instability was accepted generally during the Third Republic, except for rare periods when strong personalities, like Waldeck-Rousseau, Clemenceau, and Poincaré, succeeded in making their authority respected by the Chamber. Even during these periods of stability, the government was obliged to counter incessant intrigues hatched against it in the Parliament, and to reply to numerous challenges, which helped prevent it from exercising its full powers. The result was that instead of being the motor of a well-co-ordinated, collective, long-term action, the government found itself, during most of the Third Republic, reduced to disposing of current business, and to acting day by day, without an over-all plan, and often without real efficiency.

The very nature of a parliamentary assembly of several hundred members, such as the Chamber of Deputies, prevented it from acting as an efficient executive. But factors peculiar to French parliamentarianism impeded it as well. Individualism predominated in its mode of recruitment and function. Elected by vote for a single member only, and often not belonging to an organized party, the Deputies formed a large number of political groups in the Chamber and were rarely subject to any discipline. The regulations of the Chamber itself prevented the planning and execution of any coherent work program; some discussions went on interminably without result, others were put through so fast that no well-considered control could be exercised on the projects put to vote in the Chamber, sometimes without the text even being understood, and the order of the day, which was established in advance, could always be changed without warning, if the Chamber so decided. Also intrigues and individual combinations, often intended to get ministerial portfolios for their authors, proceeded unhindered. Political activity was sterile, having almost no connection with the needs and concerns of the country.

Even if there had been a coherent and determined majority in the Chamber, it would have met an obstacle in the Senate. The latter had legislative and political powers almost like those of the Chamber of Deputies— with the sole exception of the initiation of financial legislation. The Senate was elected indirectly by the delegates of the municipal councils, following a system which favored the small and medium-sized communes to the disadvantage of the large cities. The number of senators from each department had been set in 1884, at a time when the distribution of population gave a strong preponderance to the rural regions. Also the majority of the senators came from the zones of the traditional economy where there was an especially narrow conception of democracy and the role of the State. The aspirations of economic and social democracy, even if they had

been able to take any effective form in the Chamber, would have risked
senatorial blocking. A government trying to accomplish a program of reform to modernize the economy would have had the greatest difficulty in
obtaining the agreement of the Senate.

The political system of the Third Republic amounted to organizing a
lack of power. In the case of the Senate, it gave the impression of being
organized for the purpose of resisting democracy. The incompatability of
such a state of affairs with the exigencies of the situation created by industrial development was particularly striking after the first World War.
The destruction of the international economic balance prior to 1919 and the
deterioration of public finances, with its repercussions on the currency,
required vigorous State intervention, but France's political institutions
made effective action almost impossible. In 1926, and again in a more
permanent way between 1934 and 1940, recourse was made to décret-loi,
that is to say, to a general delegation of legislative power granted to the
government by Parliament. But this enlargement of the jurisdiction of the
government was not sufficient to obtain the authority and stability necessary
for coherent action. Moreover it had the disadvantage of accentuating
Parliament's feeling of irresponsibility, and of consolidating the idea of a
natural opposition between democracy and government. Combined with the
excessive power of a Senate which obviously represented only a minority
of the population, the décret-loi, on the other hand, aided in spreading
among the people the idea that the regime of the Third Republic was democratic only in appearance and that in reality it tended to protect the interests of the privileged classes; such conviction served as a powerful aid
to the propaganda of the Communist Party, which was hostile to the "formal
democracy" of liberal parliamentarianism.

In sum, the Third Republic, lacking authority and efficiency, was a
regime which did not seem to be truly democratic. Its government was far
too dependent on a too-powerful Chamber of Deputies which was unable to
use its power both because of the individualistic character of its electoral
origin and its organization, and because of the ability of the Senate to block
the reforms desired by the majority of the deputies.

2. Attempts to Correct the Defects of the Third Republic

The institutions of the Fourth Republic, sanctioned by the Constitution
of October 27, 1946, have had the fundamental objective of correcting the
defects of the Third Republic.

In regard to the Parliament, while the system of two chambers was
retained, a nearly absolute pre-eminence was given to the one which ema-
nated from universal suffrage, the National Assembly. Replacing the old
Senate, the Council of the Republic, whose members are elected by indirect suffrage by the delegates of the municipal councils, has only consulta-
tive powers.

The National Assembly now attempts to correct the individualism of the
old Chamber of Deputies. The most important action in this respect is not

of a constitutional nature. The replacement of the old majoritarian single-name ballot by a system of proportionate representation with a blocked list (that is to say, one in which the deputies are declared elected according to the location of their names on the list of candidates, with the voters unable to modify in this regard the parties' decisions) is originally the result of an ordinance of General de Gaulle's provisional government (August 1945). Since then it has been re-enacted with slight modifications by the electoral law of 1946.

This system of proportionate representation subordinates the deputies to the political parties on whose tickets they have been elected. It favors the well-organized large parties. As a consequence, the parliamentary groups in the National Assembly are more powerful and more disciplined than under the Third Republic. Various regulatory, or even constitutional, provisions tend to give them an important role in the organization of the Parliament.

Finally, the extension of the right to vote and of job eligibility to women—which the Senate of the Third Republic had obstinately refused them—has definitely strengthened the democratic nature of French political institutions.

The tradition according to which democracy implies the subordination of the government to the Parliament—or more exactly, to the Chamber elected by universal suffrage—has not been abandoned. This subordination has even been accentuated on some points of minor importance; thus the Assembly itself now fixes the duration of its sessions, which had formerly been ended by decree, and its Bureau controls the action of the cabinet between sessions.

The Constituent Assembly of 1946 sought to augment the authority of the government and to enlarge its capacity for efficient action. For example, during the Third Republic, the President of the Republic alone had the power to choose the Prime Minister (President of the Council). Henceforth, he only proposes him to the National Assembly, which must ratify the nomination by an absolute majority of the members. This investiture by the Assembly confers on the person of the President of the Council a particular authority. For one thing, the Assembly can hardly reverse its own decision soon after having invested him with the office; for another, it gives him authority over the ministers of his cabinet.

The Assembly can overthrow the government only under precise circumstances, by a vote obtained from a given majority, whether it be on a motion of censure or a point concerning which the government has demanded a vote of confidence after deliberation of the Council of Ministers. This vote must take place after an interval of twenty-four hours. The purpose of these rules is to prevent surprise votes due to intrigues or maneuvers, and consequently to assure ministerial stability.

Finally, the right of dissolution, which was included in the Constitution of 1875 but which had been outlawed by usage, was given again to the government by the Constitution of 1946. But the National Assembly can only be dissolved after eighteen months following its election and if two minis -

terial crises have occurred within the eighteen-month interval. In case of
dissolution the President of the National Assembly automatically replaces
the President of the Council; he must name a new Minister of Interior and
Ministers of State representing the parliamentary groups of the opposition.
All this makes the eventual exercise of the right of dissolution improbable
and difficult.

In sum, the authors of the Constitution of 1946 tried to accent the democratic character of the Republic (women's suffrage, pre-eminence of the
National Assembly), at the same time correcting parliamentary impotence,
and the lack of authority and stability of the government.

3. Operation of the Institutions of the Fourth Republic

It cannot be said that the reformed institutions of the Fourth Republic
have had the results hoped for.

The increased importance of political parties in the National Assembly
has, to be sure, put an end to some of the individualistic habits of the
Third Republic. But it has not facilitated the coherence of parliamentary
action. The jeu politique has lost much of its suppleness, since it no longer
depends on combinations of individuals. Owing to the existence of a rather
large number of important parties, the constitution of a government requires a coalition among several of them. Such a coalition is often difficult
to realize. Proportional representation adds to the difficulties. Finally,
the electoral law, which obliges the voters to choose parties, instead of
individuals, has had disastrous psychological effects. Many citizens have
the feeling that the organized political parties stand as screens between
the will of the people and the Parliament and that important decisions are
in practice handed over to the heads of parties who have no mandate from
the people. The Fourth Republic, in spite of the predominance of the National Assembly and the replacement of the Senate by a Chamber without
important powers, has therefore not succeeded in appearing really more
democratic than was the Third.

The defects which prevent the Parliament from acting efficiently are
naturally found, in an aggravated form, in the government. In spite of the
personal power which the President of the Council (Prime Minister) owes
to his investiture by the National Assembly, he must negotiate with several
parties, first to obtain this investiture, and then in order to choose his
ministers and to arrange the program of the cabinet. Any program is necessarily the result of a compromise between various and sometimes opposite
tendencies. Each minister naturally inclines to apply it, in his own sphere
of activities, in a way compatible with the particular tendencies of his
party. Everything considered, it seems that a government formed by a
coalition of parties is even less homogeneous— and therefore less capable
of coherent action— than a cabinet formed by the agreement of a certain
number of individuals.

As for ministerial stability, it is no better, after seven years, than it
was during the Third Republic. More serious still, it is evident that the

mechanisms provided by the Constitution for the mise en jeu of governmental responsibility are almost inapplicable. In general, cabinets fall because the party coalition which created them breaks out in disagreement. The efforts of the members of the Constituent Assembly to make ministerial crises less frequent are thwarted because of the role they have given to the political parties.

In short, the official institutions— National Assembly, government— today see their importance almost outweighed by the unofficial institutions, the political parties. And as those are too numerous for any one of them to be able to hold the majority, the traditional inefficiency of French political life continues to exist to a very large extent; and this, without the public even experiencing the satisfaction of finding itself confronted with a clearly democratic system.

In a State unable completely to fulfill its functions, there is a temptation for private groups to fill the void. Political power, since it is not concentrated in the hands of the State, tends to be divided among those who possess the economic means of monopolizing it. The role which is played in France today by the confederations of workers, farmers, and (to a smaller extent) owners, confirms this tendency; it almost reminds one of the feudal age. In addition, the defects of the political institutions— Parliament and government— work in favor of the administration, that is to say, the cadres of upper civil servants in whose hands what remains of public power tends to concentrate.

One can only conclude that in France today the institutions of political democracy are even less satisfactory than those of economic and social democracy.

4. Possible Reforms

Fundamentally the problem consists simply of establishing in France the bases of a true parliamentary system, with a cabinet government. The multiplicity of parties and of political tendencies, which result from the French tradition, makes this task difficult, because a cabinet government adapts itself badly to coalition. But it is not impossible.

The first reform ought to be that of the electoral system. A return to the single-name ballot of the Third Republic is perhaps not to be desired. This would tend to destroy the Communist Party (which is powerful everywhere) and confirm its followers in the belief that political liberalism is a deception. But the reapportionment could be so arranged as to reduce, without suppressing, the parliamentary representation of the political dissidents. Parliamentary work would also benefit by a numerical weakening of the Communist opposition, without excluding it altogether from political life. At the same time it would be advisable to re-establish "panachage," that is, the right of the voter to cast his ballot for the candidates appearing on the different lists, and at the same time to institute an efficient system of preferential voting, so that the order of the candidates on each list,

established by party committees, could be modified by the voters. The
first of these measures would actually bring closer together those parties
which would benefit by the ballots of the same voters; the second would
give the voters the feeling that they were truly making a sovereign decision, and not merely ratifying the choice of irresponsible committees.

(2)   It would also be advisable to modify radically the traditional rules of
French parliamentary procedure. The supremacy of the Assembly ensuing
from universal suffrage would not be called into question; but it would be
desirable that the government should be able to intervene decisively in the
establishment of the parliamentary order of the day. Thus the Assembly
would be obliged to express itself within a certain period of time on matters
considered urgent by the government, whereas today it can delay voting
indefinitely. This would also reduce the role of the parliamentary committees, which are now largely irresponsible.

The right of dissolution of the National Assembly ought to be recognized
by the government without restriction, save for the sole reservation of
the consent of the President of the Republic. In this way the government,
responsible to the National Assembly, would no longer be defenseless before it, because in serious cases it could appeal its decision to the only
sovereign that a democracy can recognize, universal suffrage.

Electoral reform would diminish without suppressing the role of parties,
and would facilitate the formation of necessary coalitions. Parliamentary
reform would replace the initiative where it ought to be, that is, in the
hands of the responsible government, with the single provision that defini-
tive decisions regarding the technical services which are today indispensable
to the preparation of the legislative texts would be left to Parliament. Governmental reform would then assure the stability and the coherence of the
exercise of power.

These three partial reforms would not modify the traditional composition
of the parliamentary institutions to which the French are more attached
than they realize. But they would permit an organization of power required
by modern conditions.

5. Conclusion

In concluding this analysis one cannot conceal the fact that at present
the realization of democratic values in France encounters obstacles which
are difficult to overcome. The most serious clearly consists of the existence of a powerful party, the Communist, which rejects the traditional
forms of liberal democracy to which the majority of the French cling. It
must not be assumed that all those who vote Communist are necessarily
Communists; on the contrary, some of them are probably moved by the
traditional distrust of government, which comes more from an elementary,
quasi-anarchical conception of democracy than from Marxist dialectic.

But the fact remains that among proletarian workers, communism has
an ardent audience, in many places a majority. These Communist followers
are in a position to launch insurrectionary strikes which imperil public

order. The experiences of 1947 and 1948 have shown that the police is equal to its task. But police action in this field is not enough. The way to fight communism successfully is to also satisfy the aspirations of the masses.

It is toward this that the institutions of economic democracy and social democracy tend. But in the realm of political democracy France has not been successful. The persistence of forces hostile to democracy, and the fears that they arouse, probably constitute the greatest obstacle to necessary changes and reforms. Nevertheless, the French democracy must be reformed; it must regain a sense of governmental authority, it must discover the value of discipline and collective productivity, it must evaluate more accurately the importance of material accomplishment, if it is going to survive in the modern world. The necessary reforms are really modest. Some day they may well be realized.

III. SOCIAL PROBLEMS AND TRENDS

1. General Behavior

In contrast to the political life, France's social life has great stability. Human relationships are reasonably constant and family ties close. Divorces, while they do occur, are not common, partly as a result of the traditional respect for the family as a basic unit of social existence and partly because of religious prohibition. This does not, of course, guarantee marital fidelity. But even infidelity does not, as a rule, disrupt the family.

Contact with kinfolk remains usually unbroken especially in the provinces. Many of the better-off urban Frenchmen acquire homes in the country, both for retirement in old age and vacation in the summer. "The base of French society," André Siegfried remarked, "always remains peasant." Nearly half of the French people who go on summer vacations (43 percent of them do) stay with relatives in the country—for one month or more. Only 20 percent go to hotels.

The café habit is strong and whole French families go to cafés frequently for a frugal drink. Nevertheless, the center of social (family) life and relaxation is the home. When they stay home evenings, the majority read or listen to the radio. Sixty-eight percent read newspapers daily. One third listen to the radio regularly, another third infrequently. Most readers are educated city men; those who read least are women, workers, and farmers. The majority of radio listeners are businessmen and professional people.

There is astonishingly little social entertainment at home. Foreigners who are sometimes hurt that their French friends or acquaintances do not invite them home might keep in mind that it is not a general national habit to do so. Only 14 percent of the French people receive at home or go visiting; 28 percent never do either. The overwhelming majority express themselves as not liking this form of entertainment.

Most of the stay-at-homes do not care for either dancing or card playing. Indeed, only 4 percent of the French people dance frequently. Three fourths of them never dance. As for card playing, 10 to 11 percent do so often; 57 percent never.

It is not, perhaps, that the French take their pleasures somberly but that they are still, to a considerable extent, a rural people. Most of them live in villages or small towns, where the ordinary metropolitan distractions are not easily available. On the farms and in the communes, moreover, there are many time-consuming chores in house and garden. This probably explains why movie attendance, on a national scale, is comparatively small: 19 percent of the French people go to the cinema once a week; 25 percent from one to three times monthly; and 47 percent never go at all. Few Frenchmen travel abroad and not many engage in sports. France is, indeed, one of the least sport-minded countries in Europe. The higher schools rarely go in for sports either. A mere 2 percent of the people say they like to watch games, mostly football. More than four fifths (81 percent) admit that they never play anything. The nearest thing to a national sport

30

is bicycling, and the grueling "Tour de France" takes place in the midst of excitement resembling the febrility of an American major league baseball season. Eight percent profess to practice cycling as a sport, as against 4 percent football and tennis playing, and 1 percent fishing and skiing. Slightly more than one fourth of the French people use the bicycle as a means of transportation. There are 11 million bicycles in France.

Possibly one reason for France's stay-at-homeness and social conservatism is the fact that, unlike her neighbor Germany, she is a woman's country. Women dominate the society both at home and behind the coulisses. The women are perhaps also the strong element in the social structure, a fact that is particularly noticeable since the defeat of 1940, when millions of men were not only subtly discredited in their traditional male role as fighters, but also imprisoned for years, so that the women had to rely more and more on their own resources.

But even before 1940 the French women set the tone of the society, as they do today. On the farms they are the laborers at least equal to men. In the tens of thousands of small shops and bistros the spirit and body behind the cash register are usually Madame. Inside the family circle it is the wife and mother who holds it together, administers the finances, and brings up the children. The spirit and taste of women have always influenced France's literature— it is the female readers who make a novelist's and poet's reputation— fashions, and even high politics. And the weaker men, instead of dominating the society with their own values, have unconsciously relinquished their position to the distaff side with their sly references to the femme and the pervasive glorification, or one might say "sexification," of amour.

The women are also an important factor where religion is concerned. Long ago the Church gave women its powerful support, in such matters as the sacredness of marriage, for example, and they in turn have rewarded it with the loyalty due to a staunch friend and consoler. The majority of the devout in France are women, and through them the Church continues to wield its influence on French life. In this matter, as in some others, the men have little to say, and they know it. Once when Jean Jaurès made an anticlerical speech and was interrupted by a heckler who ridiculed him because Mme. Jaurès was a known churchgoer, the famous Socialist leader caused gales of appreciative laughter when he retorted ironically: "My friend, no doubt you can do what you like with your wife. Not I!"

There is a great deal of discontent in France. In a survey made in the winter of 1949 slightly over half of the respondents said they were "happy enough," while one third replied "not very." In a later poll, one fourth of the respondents expressed the desire to settle abroad, as against only 4 percent of Americans who expressed a preference for leaving the United States. Nearly half of the French people find it difficult, from time to time, to fall asleep at night, and one fourth of them take sedatives or drink to induce sleep. Only the United States has a higher percentage of poor sleepers

(52 percent) than France. Despite all that, it is interesting to note that not many Frenchmen commit suicide. Paris, for instance, had only 560 suicides in 1938 and 530 in 1939. These figures have been considerably reduced since the end of the war.

The primary worry of the majority of Frenchmen (54 percent) is personal income. They are concerned with how to make ends meet, how to earn enough to buy necessities, and how to keep out of debt. A fairly substantial minority, however, is able to save money. Perhaps one third of the French people fall into this category. Comparatively few worry about taxes (only 4 percent) or international affairs (2 percent). The majority of French people concern themselves mainly with purely personal, private affairs. They live largely in a self-absorbed world.

2. Housing

World War II was tremendously costly to France in material resources. Five years of fighting, occupation, sabotage, and bombing left a swath of destruction in their wake. Whole areas lay in ruins. In all the wreckage the loss of homes and habitation was the most tragic. No fewer than 1,229,000 homes were wholly or partly destroyed. An additional 556,000 other buildings were wrecked. About 1,800 communities, 12 of them of more than 100,000 population, had to be completely rebuilt. In short, at the time of the Liberation several million Frenchmen were without proper homes.

The situation was particularly acute because there had been very little new building in France since about 1914. Wars, inflations, and enemy occupation were detrimental to construction, and this had two deleterious consequences. To protect such a basic need as shelter, successive governments froze rents at extremely low levels and, in addition, prevented evictions. This, in turn, discouraged both repairs and new construction. Nobody, obviously, wants to invest money in property over which he has no control and from which he can expect no profits.

The freezing of rents at the 1914 level, though it was inescapable, has had a paralyzing effect on the housing situation. It is ironic that, despite the fact that the cost of everything has gone up at least tenfold, the cost of lodging has gone down relatively. In 1914 a city family spent 16 percent of its income on rent; in 1924, 5 percent; and in 1944, only 4 percent. Today it is still lower. Paradoxical as it may seem, this is a catastrophe, for though the French do not pay much rent, they get very little for what they do pay.

In so far as housing is concerned, it is no exaggeration to say that a good part of France is gradually falling apart. In 1945 the average age of the buildings was fifty-seven years, 20 percent of them being over a hundred years old. In the rural areas millions live in homes without electricity or running water or gas or sewage. Even in Paris, typical of the urban centers, the situation is bad. More than 35,000 families of from three to five members live in a single room (while 25,000 bachelors or childless couples occupy five- to six-room apartments). Of the Paris homes 46 percent have no private toilets and 84 percent are without baths. Every month the Prefecture of Police announces that it must expel the tenants of some 3,000 Paris dwellings, "owing to immediate danger" of the houses "literally collapsing upon them."

This was, in fact, the expression used by Claudius Petit, former Minister of Reconstruction. In a public speech, Petit said bitterly:

> I deplore the policy of bankruptcy of the last 30 years in regard to housing. We have reached the point where our houses are falling apart faster than they are being constructed . . . I want to wrest this country from the leprosy of slums. A country that spends more for its tobacco and drinks than it does for its housing is a dying country. It is necessary that the French follow the Dutch example and devote to the building of homes not one week a year, but one week out of every four.

The average Frenchman works about two weeks in the year to pay his annual rent, while in other countries it is about twelve weeks. The French, it would appear, do not seem to put as much value on decent housing as do people in, say, Scandinavia or the United States. Thus, for example, in the year 1948 they spent a mere 30 billion francs on rent, compared to 57 billion on horse race betting, 104 billion on tobacco, and 140 billion on wine and liquor.

There are other indications of a fairly widespread, though by no means universal, indifference to being properly housed. Various polls in 1948 and 1949 showed that about one out of every four Frenchmen considered the current rents too high; three out of every four said that they were not looking for new lodgings. This is particularly strange because, according to the census of 1947, France had only 12,750,000 dwelling units and 12,900,000 families. Only 17 percent expressed a desire for a place to live, and these were mostly younger people who wanted to get married or otherwise leave the overcrowded family hearth.

What does the government do? The answer is: Something, but not much. Under pressure of a desperate minority of homeseekers, the public authorities have undertaken a public housing program at snail's pace. The Seine Housing Office has on its rolls a waiting list of 33,000 people with priority claims— those with four or more children, former war prisoners, newly wedded couples, etc. An additional 1,200 individuals with priority rights inscribe themselves every month. They will have a very long wait, indeed, for only about 3,000 units have been constructed in Greater Paris since the Liberation!

The national government has done a little more for housing than the municipalities. Between 1945 and the end of 1949 France built about 100,000 dwelling units. In view of the immensity of the need, this is not much. Claudius Petit has estimated that 300,000 dwelling units should be built

annually for thirty years. In addition, France must have at least 10,000
new classrooms every year. This would require a building program of no
less than 20,000 dwellings monthly. So far, however, the monthly construction of dwelling units has averaged a mere 1,600.

The building industry is sick. It suffers from four main shortages—
materials, labor, modern techniques, and money. Although the materials
situation has greatly improved, that of labor, methods, and money has not.
In all of France there are only around 400,000 construction workers, and
the immediate need is for at least twice that number. The problem of outmoded building techniques, as a result of the virtual absence of competition
in construction, is particularly grave. Thus, while the building of a four-
room house requires 4,000 work-hours in the United States and 7,000 in
Great Britain, it takes 25,000 in France!

The financial problem involved is also serious. Since 1914 building costs
have gone up from sixty to eighty times. This necessitates an astronomical
outlay of cash, and since no private entrepreneur can be expected to invest
money in rent-frozen and low-rent buildings, assuming that they had the
funds to do so, it follows that either the rents must be unfrozen or the government must enter the field of large-scale low-cost housing.

Some steps have already been taken in this direction. A law passed in
September 1948, which went into effect in Janaury 1949, called for a re-
valuation of rents, providing that, within five years, rents for workers'
housing could reach 12 percent of minimum wage. This is something of a
revolution, since today the worker spends a mere 3 to 4 percent of his earnings on rent.

It is no exaggeration to say that the future health and well-being of
France may depend upon the success of this law. If by balancing rents and
the cost of living a large market for construction could be created, it may
lead to a lowering of building costs and a modernization of the construction
industry. It would then also be possible to follow the British or Scandinavian
pattern of creating a kind of "public utility" in low-rent housing.

For the time being, however, the future of housing is poor. France's
1950 budget provides for 37 billion francs for the construction of "inex-
pensive dwellings" and 420 billions for military purposes. In other words,
France will spend almost twelve times more on the armed forces than on
housing— 18 percent of the budget for military expenditures and 1.6 percent
on homes. The current budget absorbs up to 40 percent for military expenditures, which means that housing must again be neglected.

There seem to be only two ways to solve the catastrophic housing situation. One is for the government to encourage private construction by un-
freezing rents on the new buildings and by guaranteeing a minimum return
on the investment. This would run into sharp political opposition from the
radical parties, but it is hard to see how any responsible government can
in the long run avoid taking that risk. Another way, which is much the harder,
is to undertake a systematic change in the national psychology regarding
the desirability and, indeed, the vital necessity of decent homes. In the last

analysis, comfortable, healthful, and modern housing is the product of a desire to have it. If there is no deeply felt need, there will be no widespread supply.

For a modern society low-standard housing can become tragically expensive— in health, in welfare, in civic standards. France cannot afford the luxury of slums and primitive homes. Somehow, she must create a national preference for good homes with modern facilities; a demand for decent housing, if it permeated a sizable portion of the nation, would stimulate the proper action to bring it into being. It would also reinvigorate the whole spirit of enterprise, optimism, and modernism so sadly lacking now.

3. The Demographic Problem

In recent years French leaders have come to realize that if their country's rate of reproduction remained unchanged, France would cease to be a major nation in three or four generations. The population of Greater Paris, one scientist estimated, would be reduced from roughly 5 million in 1940 to about 1 million a century later. The rest of the French population would decline more or less in the same proportion until, around the middle of the next century, France would be not much more populous than Sweden. This may be an exaggeration, but it illustrates the point graphically.

The demographic decline began long ago.

When George Washington was sworn in as President of about 4 million Americans, France had more people than any other state in Europe, except Russia. At the beginning of the Revolution of 1789 there were some 25 million Frenchmen, or about one seventh of Europe's total. Soon after the middle of the nineteenth century the French population virtually stopped increasing. It became stationary at, roughly, the 40-million point. This was the period when France's immediate neighbors, Germany and Italy, started the process of eventually doubling their populations. Between 1861 and 1865 there were thirty-eight more births than deaths for every 10,000 Frenchmen. This fell to eleven in 1906–10, to eight in 1931–35, and to three in 1936–37. Until 1946 deaths exceeded births. On the eve of World War II France was, from a demographic point of view, a dying country.

In relation to other powers, France's decline was even more drastic. Napoleon's France contained 15.2 percent of the people of Europe; today's France, about half that.

Among the main causes of the population decline have been urbanization and war.

Up to the end of the nineteenth century France was largely rural. In the middle of that century three fourths of the people lived in the country; today, less than half. About 53 percent of the French people now live in urban areas.

This has meant a diminution in the number of children. While country

folk usually had large families, city people have preferred small ones.
Poor Frenchmen, particularly workers, could never afford many children.
Wretched housing generally mitigated against large families. A recent study
of a working-class community showed that 18 percent of the families had
no children, 19 percent had one child, 22 percent had two children, and
only 11 percent had three. In a survey made in 1947 France's working class
indicated the least desire for large families.

The educated and anticlerical bourgeoisie is likewise not devoted to big
families. Some do not want many children because they fear a decrease
of their living standards; others, particularly those with fixed salaries,
because they cannot afford them. This is strikingly true, for instance, of
the civil servants, including teachers. About 39 percent of the government
employees are unmarried and 30 percent are childless. One fourth of the
married couples have only one child.

One must emphasize that inherently urbanization, as such, need not lead
to a decline in population. It is only when urbanization is accompanied by
slums, disease, and miserable living conditions in general that it tends to
lead to depopulation.

War has been another factor in France's demographic decline. World
War I cost France 1,320,000 in killed and more than 700,000 in crippled.
This loss was felt with particular severity because it involved men in the
reproductive age. More than half (57 percent) of those killed were under
thirty-one years old. The direct loss of around 2 million men, out of a
total male population of some 20 million, was probably the greatest single
catastrophe that has befallen France in recent centuries.

World War II further depleted the French population. (See also Chapter
V, Section 1.) The Germans captured around 1,800,000 prisoners— one
third of all Frenchmen between the ages of twenty and fifty— and kept most
of them prisoner for five years. This prevented natural reproduction and
resulted in a sharp drop in the birth rate. The following is the French government's list of human losses in the period between 1939 and 1945:

Excess of deaths over births	550,000
Military casualties, 1939—40	130,000
Military casualties, 1940—45	60,000
Civilians killed as a result of the war	120,000
Civilians shot or massacred	40,000
Died in Germany	300,000
Total	1,200,000

In addition, 410,000 were wounded. Altogether, World War II cost
France 3 percent of her population.

This blood-letting of the two world wars has had a profound effect upon
the whole French society. The mass killing of France's youth not only left
what one French scientist has characterized as a "biologic hole" in the
nation, but also deprived it of a reservoir of potential leaders, thinkers,
creators, and skilled workers.

The demographic effect of World War II will not be felt acutely until around 1960; but the losses did help to focus public attention on France's plight. After the Liberation, the French government did take a number of steps to overcome the nation's grave and fundamental weakness.

In April 1945 France set up a General Secretariat of Family and Population, which was soon placed under the Ministry of Public Health and Population. The Ministry then created a National Institute of Demographic Studies, for, strange as it may seem, France possessed no organized body of scientific data on the subject that was causing her creeping death. The National Institute is now carrying on basic research on the whole range of subjects connected with population— biological, medical, economic, psychiatric, social, and statistical.

> It is an organism of research and diffusion. It studies the problems of population under the double aspect of quantity and quality. Its field of activity is not limited to the gathering and comparison of statistics. None of the human sciences is alien to it; and, in its various sections, it calls on history, geography, ethnography, economics, biology, psychology and comparative law.[12]

The National Institute, directed by the demographer Alfred Sauvy, has semiautonomous status under the Ministry. Its staff of scientists is among the best of France. The Institute publishes a quarterly, Population, and special studies under the title Travaux et Documents. These publications help to spread knowledge and to educate the French people on the country's demographic problems and needs.

The Institute is more than a clearing house for ideas and for their diffusion. It also co-operates with government agencies in the making of policies. To halt the ravages of alcoholism, for example, the Institute has recently proposed the establishment of "Centers of Re-education" as cure stations, wherein alcoholics would be given six-month treatments. So far, however, the National Assembly has proceeded cautiously, for public opinion is not yet ripe for drastic action. One of the Institute's main, and perhaps most difficult, tasks is to enlighten French public opinion— a slow process in a country of extreme individualism and where the press is generally more tendentious than objective.

Since the Liberation there has been a steady increase in the number of marriages, as well as a growth in the birth rate, both of which are systematically encouraged by the government. But in the meantime the need for more people, that is, adults, has remained urgent, not only for purposes of natural reproduction, but also for economic production. For France has an aging population and a severe shortage of labor, particularly skilled workers. The old and unproductive people are a steadily growing burden on the young. On an average, five productive adults have to work to support three nonworking aged. In a few years the proportion is expected to be five to four. Owing to this shortage of male labor, France has one of the highest rates of employed women in Europe. In 1931 one out of every four women worked for a living, a proportion that is roughly still true today.

It will be asked, why does not France encourage immigration to fill the biologic and economic gaps? The answer is that such efforts have been made. Indeed, France has long been an immigrant-absorbing country, the largest in Europe. Without immigration, the French population would have been considerably lower than the 40-million point. Between 1921 and 1931, for example, immigrants entered France at the average annual rate of 200,000. On the eve of World War II France had more than 3 million foreigners (Italians, Spaniards, Poles, Belgians, etc.).

But this sporadic and unorganized immigration was a mere stopgap. It just helped to hold the population line fixed. After the Liberation the government undertook a policy of planned immigration and the encouragement of naturalization. A new Code of French Nationality was passed in October 1945, making naturalization easier than before. In 1947 there were about 300,000 applications for citizenship, of which one third were expected to go through.

In November 1945 a National Office of Immigration was set up in the Ministry of Labor and Social Security. It was to operate closely with the Ministry of Public Health and Population.

Some population specialists, thinking in long-range terms, thought that France needed at least 5 million immigrants. Others, notably those representing the Four-Year Monnet Plan, hoped to get 650,000 immigrant workers by 1950. As it turned out, both groups were way off the mark.

The first difficulty to overcome was basic: Where was France to get the proper immigrants? At the end of the war there existed four potential sources of manpower—the DP camps, the North Africans, Germans, and Italians. For a number of reasons, including international-political, the DPs were not considered acceptable. The North Africans, especially Algerians, were coming into France freely anyhow. In 1949 there were about 100,000 of them in Paris alone, mostly from the bottom of the Algerian social scale. Many of them now indulge in petty racketeering and add to the general crime rate. But worst of all, they are unskilled, uneducated, and neither easily assimilable culturally nor adjustable industrially. As for Germans, for obvious political reasons large-scale immigration could not be organized; French public opinion is still bitter against the Boche. (See Chapter V, Section 3.) Even so, after 1945 the French did try to encourage German prisoners of war to remain in the country as civilian workers. About 123,000 did so, and some even married French women, but most have since returned to Germany.

Italy alone was thus left as a reservoir of human resources. In March 1947, after long and strained negotiations, the French and Italian governments made an agreement for 200,000 immigrants to come to France that year. The Italians were to enjoy the same rights, wages, and privileges as French workers. They would join whatever trade union they liked. They were permitted to send 40 percent of their earnings to their families in Italy. When their one-year contract expired, they had the right to renew it, and ultimately, if they wished, to become French citizens.

But the policy of bringing in Italians was wrecked by administrative bungling and international misunderstanding. Disregarding Italian psychology, French officials treated the immigrants at best as conscript and at worst as prisoners. Italians and Frenchmen have, indeed long been antipathetic — Italians tending to regard the French as "immoral" and decadent, and French making fun of Italians as "spaghettis." Mussolini's "stab in the back" at a time of France's deepest humiliation was hardly calculated to endear Italians to the French. Such memories are apt to linger. At any rate, Italians who signed up to work in France were not only pushed around and often beaten by French officials but were never told where they were being sent and what was expected of them. Many of them, furthermore, found the damp climate in certain regions of France unbearable. Others disliked the food. Most of them were poorly housed, which was inevitable in view of France's housing situation. Word about these difficulties quickly spread in Italy, with the result that only 76,000 entered France in 1947. But one third of them returned home. In the end, Italian immigration, a necessity both for overpopulated Italy and underpopulated France, practically dried up.

At the end of 1948 only 79,403 immigrants, mostly Italians, Germans, and seasonal Belgians, were working in France. The bulk of them were in agriculture, and large numbers in mining.

4. Social Security[13]*

In matters of social legislation, public health, and the general protection and welfare of the poor and dependent, France has been, until recently, one of the more backward countries in Europe. What social legislation did exist was grudging and limited. A ten-hour working day was introduced in 1904; certain invalid and old-age insurance was partly provided for in 1910. In 1930 the social insurance system was regorganized, but it remained circumscribed and inadequate.

The Popular Front of 1936–37, led by the Socialist Premier Léon Blum, tried to catch up with France's social backwardness and to give the working people a stake and interest in the economy. A whole series of social reforms was introduced, and never had France made so much social progress in so brief a time. Among the many reforms were holidays with pay, for the first time in French history, a universal forty-eight hour work week without loss of wages; collective bargaining; the raising of the school-leaving age; and the improvement in the social insurance system.

These reforms aroused a storm of opposition on the part of the conservative elements, aided by the Fascists, both native and foreign. Furthermore, the international situation became increasingly grave. The success of Franco in Spain and the openly hostile moves of Hitler and Mussolini gave the French Republic the jitters and scared the public into abandoning further reforms. Intrigue and fear led to the overthrow of the Popular Front. At any rate, the social reforms were too little and came too late; within two years after the fall of Blum, France was at war.

*Based on a paper, in MS, by Louis Rosenstock-Franck.

In all that period the health of the nation had been especially neglected. Diseases, notably tuberculosis, flourished in the slums and ravaged the poor strata of the population. In recent years, however, a good deal of progress has been made, especially in preventive and prophylactic medicine. Since 1942 a medical declaration of venereal disease has been compulsory. There is large-scale vaccination against tuberculosis. There are a number of antituberculous and antivenereal dispensaries, where the patient, sent by his doctor, is examined by a specialist and then advised as to the proper treatment. These antituberculous and antivenereal movements have recently been extended to the protection of mothers, babies, and children. In schools, shops, and offices examinations for tuberculosis are compulsory.

Today France has 2,114 public health institutions, with a total of 322,000 hospital and hospice beds. This makes an average of one bed per 300 persons, as against an American average of one per 100. Many of the hospitals, however, are out of date and poorly equipped.

It is interesting to note the evolution of the number of doctors, dentists, and pharmacists since the turn of the century.

	Physicians	Dentists	Pharmacists
1901	1 per 2,450 persons	1 per 21,800 persons	1 per 3,800 persons
1937	1 per 1,620	1 per 4,900	1 per 3,500

Thus, while France's population remained relatively unchanged in this period, considerable progress was made in the field of medical personnel. The number of doctors increased by about 50 percent and that of dentists more than quadrupled. Nevertheless, it should be kept in mind that the progress was small compared to the United States, for example, where there are at least twice as many doctors per capita as in France.

In this respect it should be noted that there is a difference in attitude toward matters medical between a Frenchman and, say, an American. Examinations and general checkups are not as common in France as in the United States among the same social strata. An American is inclined to feel that he owes good health not only to himself but also to his group, that his health is a part of the disciplines which society has normally a right to expect from him; a Frenchman, however, feels that his health is a purely individual concern and entirely his personal responsibility. This helps to explain why the French Social Security system differs from the British or Russian, for example. In France a person insured under Social Security has the right to choose his own physician.

The strictly private character of "individual health" comes out fully in the complex feelings of most Frenchmen toward hospitals. The French hospital today still bears the marks of its origins, that is to say, an institution set up for the purpose of lodging rather than treating the poor, the aged, and the crippled. In no French hospital, for example, does the portion

allotted to medical and pharmaceutical expenses go beyond 50 percent of
the daily costs. A hospital is, in essence, a poor man's shelter rather
than an institution for medical treatment. Hence the Frenchman has a
traditional aversion for hospitals, where the whole atmosphere implies a
kind of degradation, a public confession of individual destitution. Some
of the newer hospitals, to be sure, have a more modern, more American-
like appearance, but too many still remain grim and forbidding, their
leprous appearance imbuing the patient with the feeling that he would only
leave feet first. Psychologically speaking, the Frenchman may be said to
be at war with his hospitals.

For a long time orphans and illegitimate children were largely neglected
by an individualistic society that left such troublesome problems to the
caprice of private charity. This was particularly grave, owing to the high
rate of illegitimacy. Over the ten-year period 1930–39 the annual average
of illegitimacy was as high as 16 percent. In other words, one out of six
children was without acknowledged parentage and, consequently, without
proper security and protection. Thousands of neglected infants and children
died in slummy foundling homes and other eleemosynary institutions.

Venereal diseases and abortions tended further to cut down the health
and numbers of the population. Although houses of prostitution have been
closed since the Liberation, venereal diseases have not noticeably decreased.
Incidentally, at least one third of the French people think that there has
been an increase in prostitution since the closing of the brothels and they
feel that they should be reopened. Another third believe that the closing
has made no difference one way or another. Most newspaper readers feel
that the houses should be opened up again.

As for abortions, despite the fact that both abortionist and abortee are
subject to imprisonment and fines, they are not uncommon, especially for
those who can afford the price. In the summer of 1949 no fewer than 150
aborted women, together with two midwives who assisted in the operations,
were tried in a Paris court and given stiff sentences. One of the midwives
was sentenced to three years in prison, 25,000 francs fine, and depriva-
tion of her license for twenty years; the other was sent to jail for one year
and fined 10,000 francs. The patients were fined up to 8,000 francs each
and given eight-month suspended prison sentences. Even more severe laws
are now being contemplated.

As if to catch up for lost time in matters of health and social progress,
the French have passed a whole series of major social security acts since
the Liberation. This legislation, which is still being augmented, has given
France one of the most impressive and extensive social security systems
in the democratic world. Sécurité Sociale covers all persons who work for
their living, and their offspring— a total of about 18 million individuals,
or close to half the nation.

For a small fraction of their deducted pay— 6 percent of pay below a
certain ceiling— [14] France's wage and salary earners who are insured
under Sécurité Sociale get a wide variety of benefits. Social Security pro-

tects workers, children, pregnant mothers, families, the indigent, and the aged. It is an extremely complicated system of graded rates. Invalids, for example, get both an indemnity and, if totally incapacitated, 40 percent of their average salary. Widows receive half the pensions of their husbands, and men past sixty up to 40 percent of their base pay, depending upon their residence, location, etc. Injured workers get from one-half to two-thirds of their wages while sick, as well as completely free medical, surgical, hospital, and prosthetic services. Social Security also pays 80 percent of medical and hospital expenses, including drugs, of all those who are insured under it.

In July 1949 a conservative Paris publication, after one of its customary attacks on Social Security (as wasteful and burdensome on the taxpayer), received the following letter from one indignant reader:

> You people are trying to discredit Social Security. I am a simple salaried man, earning 14,000 francs [about $42] monthly, plus 7,900 francs in family allowances, since I have two children. In four years of marriage I often had need for a doctor. In our family we have had two confinements, whooping cough, a double pneumonia, an intestinal infection, my wife had serious anemia, and there was an appendix operation . . . Naturally I had to deal with Social Security, of which I am an ardent defender, for without it my financial situation would be catastrophic. To give you one case: My wife's appendectomy. It cost 31,119 francs [about $95]. Social Security reimbursed me 19,355; I had to pay only 11,764. I can't call that expensive. Before the War we had no such advantages.

Motherhood, in particular, is given every assistance under Social Security. Maternity benefits include complete medical expenses, free delivery, free milk, three-months pay, and large premiums for each child, ranging from two to three times the parent's monthly wage (20 percent of the average salary for the second child; 30 percent more for each additional child). Thus an industrial worker earning, say, 15,000 francs a month gets an outright gift of 45,000 francs for his first child and 30,000 francs for each additional child. Even after the delivery and the premiums, there are continuing benefits. An employee's wage or salary is scaled upward in proportion to the number of children he has, and there are, in addition, delicately graded allocations for rent.

Recently Social Security added a few more benefits. In the summer of 1949 nonsalaried professional persons in retirement were allowed 19,200 francs annually. At the same time the National Assembly created another category of beneficiaries, "the economically weak." About 2 million people fall into this category. They include persons past the age of sixty, the infirm, the incurable, and the salaried old workers with insufficient income. All these "economically weak" are given cards which entitle them to (1) an annual round trip on the national railroads anywhere in France;

(2) free medical service; (3) free legal service; and (4) certain reductions in prices and rates, for such things as radio tax, gas, and electricity. The Social Security system is under attack on the part of conservatives and the Right-wing press. The main criticisms leveled against it are that, first, the national economy cannot afford the burden, and second, it is wastefully administered. Critics point out that it absorbs 5.6 percent of the national income and that its administrative cost has more than tripled between 1947 and 1948— from 9,925,000,000 francs to 20,785,000,000.

Defenders of the system deny the charge of waste or really serious inefficiency. They point out that Social Security is a mammoth affair, a kind of "big business" in its own way. In 1947 the system had an income of 195,891,000,000 francs and in 1948, 332,442,000,000. These are, indeed, somewhat astronomical figures and one can hardly expect them to be handled with absolute precision. In 1948 Social Security paid out a total of 325,196,000,000 francs [slightly under 1 billion dollars] in benefits. It had a surplus of 19 billion francs left in its treasury. That, Social Security's champions say, cannot be called inefficiency.

As for the accusation of burdensomeness on the national economy, that seems to have little relevance under modern conditions. The truth is that Social Security spreads purchasing power, assists the "economically weak," and serves as a stabilizing force throughout the whole population. Psychologically, moreover, it is of decisive importance. Without it, large sections of the people would go to pieces morally, not to mention materially. At any rate, the Social Security system has registered many successes since its inception. Infant mortality, for instance, has decreased by two-thirds between 1938 and 1947. Tuberculosis has also declined sharply. In 1936 the tuberculosis death rate was 10.5 per 10,000 inhabitants; during World War II it increased to 15 or 16, but in 1946 the rate dropped to 8. The rate is still falling, but there still exists a shortage of sanatoria and preventoria.

CAUSES OF DEATH, 1948
(506,277 Recorded Deaths)

Heart and circulatory system diseases of	100,419
Cancer	70,864
Nervous system diseases, cerebral hemorrhages	68,007
Respiratory diseases (excluding tuberculosis)	48,013
Old age	38,502
Tuberculosis	31,030
Digestive diseases	26,166
Infectious diseases	10,033
Other suicides and accidents	26,408
Infantile diseases	14,024
Others	72,811
Total	506,277

The most striking gains have been in the birth rate. The turning point in this respect came in 1946, when 835,000 babies were born. This was 335,000 more than the annual average in the last seventy-five years. At the same time the death rate also fell, from 155 per 10,000 in 1939 to 122 in 1948. The excess of births over deaths has been continuing ever since. In 1948 there were 864,000 births, as against 506,000 deaths. Today, for the first time in her history, France has a population of over 42 million.

The Social Security system, in sum, has given the national life firmness and a measure of stability which have been needed for a long time. It is now deeply rooted in the needs and loyalties of the people.

IV. MATERIAL CONDITIONS

1. Historic Background of the Economy

Professor Raymond Aron, one of France's leading scholars, has written:

> The root of all the troubles from which France is suffering is
> her inadequate production: she no longer produces enough goods
> and services to satisfy the demands of her population. This dispro-
> portion between goods in demand and goods supplied is, in essence,
> due to the slow rate at which output and productive capacity have
> advanced since the beginning of the present century and, above all,
> since the war of 1914. It is obvious that the destruction caused by
> the war and the extensive pillaging of French property by the
> Nazis have aggravated this disproportion, but signs of a crisis were
> obvious before 1939. It would be false to hold the recent destructive
> war and the rapacity of the occupant entirely responsible for this
> state of affairs.

A brief historic summary of the French economy is in order. France
is rich in regard to land and resources. Among European states only the
Soviet Union exceeds her in size and potential wealth. France's population
density—76 persons per square kilometer—is one of the lowest in Europe.
Paradoxically, this low density is, at the same time, an index of actual
weakness and a mark of potential strength.

Although poor in coal, France outranks Western European countries
in the possession of ore, especially in Lorraine. Her known reserves of
iron ore are 181 tons per capita, as compared to 122 for the United King-
dom and 19 for Germany.

The extent of cultivable land per capita is higher than that of any other
country in Western Europe. The land, moreover, is generally fertile, and
though there has been little scientific agriculture, France has been self-
sufficient in food for a long time. Bread, dairy products, fruit, vegetables,
meat, fish, and wine have been abundant and usually cheap. Except in
periods of wars and other crises, Frenchmen, even the poorer classes,
have been accustomed to eating and drinking well.

On the face of it, France was ripe for industrialization. She possessed
the means for the attainment of a high degree of industrialization and mechanization, and it is, indeed, a matter of surprise that she did not fully
achieve it. (See also Chapter II, Sections 3 and 5.) The country had an
abundance of food, a good transportation network (roads, railroads, and
canals), excellent harbors and docks, a skilled working class, an intelli-
gent public, and a first-rate educational system. But despite all that, industrialization and productivity have lagged far behind France's immediate
neighbors—Germany and Great Britain.

One explanation, as André Siegfried has pointed out, is that France has
been essentially rural-minded and largely individualistic. Business was,
by preference, small-scale and often family-owned. Psychologically, the

spirit of big risk and plunging, so characteristic of American enterprise, has been lacking in France. Although there has been a certain amount of Big Business in France, French businessmen as a rule preferred to play it safe. [15]

French capitalism has been characterized by two main aspects. One was the tendency to invest abroad rather than at home; the other, the comparative inefficiency of the industrial system.

Instead of investing boldly in new business ventures, or indulging in speculative enterprises, French capital has been inclined to seek what seemed to be "safe" outlets in foreign countries. This turned out to be short-sighted. It had a number of unfortunate consequences, both personal and national.

In the first place, French citizens often lost billions of their foreign-invested francs when upheavals occurred abroad. In the second place, the flight of capital kept France comparatively underindustrialized and technologically unprogressive. Finally, the habit of investing abroad created an idle capitalist class with a "coupon clipping" petty bourgeois mentality and without a sense of civic or national responsibility.

This type of capitalist mind, so essentially different from the far-ranging and experimental American business spirit, exacerbated the long-smoldering class conflict in France. It made the penny-saving, penny-conscious capitalist distrust the worker, and the worker in turn hate the rich. Labor resented the fact that the capitalist grew wealthy without working. The capitalist was convinced that the worker was envious of his luxury and was only waiting for a chance to expropriate him—as was taught in Syndicalist and, later, Communist theory. Such a prevailing state of mind had a further depressing effect on the spirit of business enterprise. Why risk your money, many a wealthy man asked himself, when there is always the danger that a demagogic government dominated by the poor might confiscate your property, or at least cut down your profits?

Hence the tendency for "safe" foreign investments, which increased faster than the national income. Between 1890 and 1899 France's national income was 27 billion francs annually; but between 1890 and 1902 foreign investments almost doubled—from 20 billion francs to around 37 billion. By 1914 French citizens had from 45 to 50 billion francs invested abroad, or the equivalent of about 9 to 10 billion gold dollars.

2. Economic Consequences of World War I

Unlike some preceding wars, that of 1914—18 changed economic and social conditions. The devastation of ten departments of France, the heavy increase of the public debt, the devaluation of the currency by four-fifths, the repudiation of the Russian debt and, above all, the 2 million casualties which the country suffered, all these threw the social-economic structure out of gear.

From 1890 to 1914 France had patiently woven the network of the Triple

Alliance, aimed at containing the pressure of the Berlin-Vienna axis. After World War I, having vainly tried to base her security on a military superiority which neither her demography nor the other great powers (particularly Great Britain) would allow, France rested her hope for security in the League of Nations and in a close alliance with governments created or strengthened by the Versailles Treaty, notably Poland, Czechoslovakia, Roumania, and Yugoslavia. From 1934 on, faced by the rising tide of Nazism, France reverted to the traditional Franco-Russian alliance. France's desperate search for international security was also reflected in the construction of the purely defensive (and incomplete) Maginot Line.

This search for security was expensive. From 1919 to 1939 military expenditures— both pensions and debts of World War I and military preparations for the future— heavily drained the national income and correspondingly limited productive expenditures, as well as social and educational ones. In 1936, 61 percent of the total budget of 77 billion francs was expended on national defense and the public debt, 26 percent on productive and administrative expenses, 7 percent on social welfare, and 6 percent on education.

Before World War I France was, next to Great Britain, the great creditor nation in the world. Like Great Britain, France represented the prototype of a country of long-established wealth, with a relatively high standard of living, buying more than selling, but covering its commercial deficit by indirect exports and income from foreign investments.

World War I reduced France's foreign investment to between 18 and 20 billion gold francs. These investments were usually in the form of nonspeculative stable securities. It is significant that very little of this money— a mere one-tenth— was invested in France's own colonies. Frenchmen seemed to have more confidence in the Americas, Asia, and non-French Africa than in their own colonies.

Two-thirds of the foreign investments were public securities guaranteed by the borrowing nations. One-fourth was made up of railroad, mines, and bank securities. Less than 10 percent of the total represented strictly industrial shares. Unlike his British neighbor, the French investor did not have his investment supervised by agents sent to the spot, or by branch banks established abroad, or by his own children employed as directors or engineers in foreign factories. Instead, he invested in what he regarded as "the surest thing" and which generally fitted the French government's foreign policy.

3. Distribution of Occupations

On the eve of World War II more than one third of France's working population centered its economic activities in agriculture, while a little over one third made its living in industry and transportation.

The workers were distributed by social categories as follows: managers, manual and clerical employees, and unattached laborers (small craftsmen or workers at home):

	Working Population	Active Agricultural Population	Active Non-agricultural Population
Heads of establishments (managers)	28.8%	61.4%	11.2%
Employees	13.5	--	21.5
Workers	42.3	27.5	50.2
Independents	15.4	11.1	17.1

If one takes into account that many "managers" can be found in the "independent" category, one may assume that at least 30 percent of the active pre-World War II population was made up of the former—ranging from the operator of a large undertaking employing thousands of workers to the single independent operator. The figures are particularly significant

FRANCE'S WORKING POPULATION, 1939
(Total number 21.6 million)

Occupation	Working Population
Agriculture, forestry	35.3%
Mining	2.0
Manufacturing	31.7
Transportation	5.0
Commerce	12.5
Professional, religious	3.0
Government officials	6.7
Domestic and other services	3.8

in the case of agriculture, where more than 60 percent of the working population were included as "managers," that is to say, running their own enterprises. Whether the agricultural "manager" was an owner (75 percent of the cases), a farmer renting his farm (20 percent), or a share-cropper (5 percent), his psychology was more akin to that of the "owner" than that of the "proletarian" on a payroll. In general, agricultural France was and is a country of landowners whose relatively small properties (75 percent of them less than 25 acres) are cultivated by the owner with the help of his family.

Besides agriculture, the percentage of the working population considered as "managers"—independent craftsmen, "small bosses," etc. — was around 20 percent. In other words, no less than three fourths of France's active working population made its living in relative independence. This is still largely true today.

4. The Psychology of the Independents

These independents, whether industrial producers, farmers, or craftsmen, are passionately devoted to individual property—the symbol of their independence— and to political security. To explain the extent of this feeling, it would be necessary to go back to the French Revolution of 1789, which redistributed ecclesiastical and seignioral lands and brought political liberty to Frenchmen.

As the mainstay of individual, and therefore familial, security, French private property is carefully husbanded, defended, and bequeathed. It is not gambled away on distant projects. It is defended against collectivist movements and is transmitted to heirs. Gifts to charity, to museums and universities, to laboratories and other institutions, so characteristic of the American society, are rare in France. The welfare of the public lies more in the realm of the State and the bureaucracy than in private generosity.

5. Underindustrialization

Today France has few really big plants. Industrial goods are fabricated largely in small and medium-sized establishments. This has some advantages, such as a measure of skilled handwork and relative stability. But for the national prosperity and strength as a whole, the small-plant system has certain drawbacks.

A mark of the weakness of the French economy has been its comparatively low productivity, both in industry and in agriculture, the latter of which employs 40 percent of the working population. France's relative economic inefficiency has been due largely to insufficient mechanization and technological underdevelopment.

The Rapport Général sur le Premier Plan de Modernisation (November 1946— January 1947) stated the situation in blunt terms:

> On the eve of the second World War, nearly a third of our capacity of industrial production was idle. The spirit of enterprise was so weakened that investments barely covered depreciation. The output of labor, whether in agriculture or industry, was far lower than in countries with modern equipment. Due to our lesser efficiency, as well as unemployment, take-home pay and the standard of living were clearly inferior in France to those in other countries. However mediocre, this standard of living was not even sustained out of current production: for 20 to 25 percent of our purchases abroad we were paying with the income from foreign investments. In other words, we were living on the savings of the preceding generations.

It should be pointed out that the technical ability of French workers is in no way inferior to those of their West European neighbors. But the organization of production is too often outdated to permit labor to be as efficient and productive as in the United States or Great Britain. Before World War II a French worker produced about one-third of that of an American and two-thirds of that of a British one.

PRE-WORLD WAR II OUTPUT PER MAN
IN FRANCE AND OTHER COUNTRIES*

Country	Last Known Year	Output per Man (I. U.)
New Zealand	1937	1,702
United States	1937	1,485
Canada	1936	1,352
Great Britain	1937	1,275
Australia	1937	1,212
Switzerland	1930	1,036
Germany	1937	828
Sweden	1936	804
Norway	1937	705
Denmark	1933	679
Holland	1934	662
France	1934	641

*Taken from the table facing p. 148 of Colin Clark, The Conditions of Economic Progress (London: Macmillan and Co., 1940).

This is particularly illustrated in the coal mines. Between 1925 and 1938 the average output per man shift in France (excluding the Saar) was 0.733 tons, as against 1.410 tons in the Ruhr, 1.087 in Britain, and 4.25 (bituminous) in the United States. In other words, French miners were about half as productive as German ones and only one-sixth as productive as American ones.

A French engineer has estimated that in 1929, a year of virtually unchecked free enterprise, the price of both industrial and agricultural products was, in terms of units of labor, three to four times higher than in America. He gave the following comparative figures:[16]

	France	U.S.	Difference
Price of wheat, per quintal (in number of days of work)	7	2	350%
Price of pork, per quintal (in number of days of work)	43	11	400%
Price of steel, per ton (in hours of work)	147	60	250%
Price of aluminum, per ton (in hours of work)	2,200	760	300%

6. Inefficient Distribution

An economy based upon personal-individual enterprise and mainly small-scale production could not be hospitable to the modern techniques of distribution, particularly as developed in the United States.

In France commerce has not kept pace with the modern tendency toward centralization. The new forms of distribution— large stores, chain stores,

emporia— which are less developed in France than in other European
countries, have been hampered by restrictive legislation and by punitive
taxes. In addition, too often the individualism of the small merchants and
their lack of commercial education have prevented them from uniting in
buyers' co-operatives or in "chains of distribution."

There has been, indeed, a tendency to increase the number of small
businessmen and petty enterprises. This was partly stimulated by the
existence of the black market during and soon after World War II.

The French government has discouraged the more modern and cheaper
means of distribution for reasons of political psychology— to protect small
business. A law passed in March 1936 forbade the opening up of new emporia. Another law, that of October 1935, forbade the circulation of
"truck-bazaars" which sold a wide assortment of goods in the rural areas.
These trucks were a serious threat to small-town tradesmen, since they
not only brought goods to the consumer but also sold them cheaper.

The financial policy of the government discriminates against business
combinations and chain stores. It gives many advantages to small business.
In some instances (the law of March 22, 1936, in regard to shoes) the
State has been known to prevent the opening of new stores in order to slow
down competition and stop a decline in prices.

A few recent attempts at self-service stores have not yet met with
much success. The problem is, among other things, psychological. To
the French housewife, shopping is not merely a daily chore but also a
distraction, a pleasant outlet for her leisure. For many housewives shopping represents an opportunity to acquire the latest gossip and information; the shop or market place may be considered the news agency of the
town or neighborhood. The advantages of self-service stores could no
more make up for their uninteresting uniformity than canned soups could
take the place, for the French, of homemade ones based on individual
and time-honored recipes.

For similar reasons all experts unanimously agree on the failure of
the sale of utility goods in France. From 1945 to 1948 large-scale plans
for the sale of shoes, linen, bedding, and furniture of good quality and
standard make were launched. The result was a complete failure. It
should be noted that similar efforts met with great success in Britain.
Even during the period of the worst shortages, French consumers refused
to consent to have the government decide what they should buy.

All these trends reflect both the intractable individualism of the French
and the practices of an outmoded country that is afraid of risk and of progress. A veritable revolution will be necessary to bring France's business
practices up to date.

7. Reconstruction and the Monnet Plan

France's already weak economy suffered near-paralyzing blows during
the war and the German occupation. The Germans not only looted and

requisitioned, but they also drained the public finances by imposing an occupation cost of 282 billion francs. Bombing and fighting caused vast destruction of the material resources. Approximately 18 percent of France's real property was destroyed or damaged. A total of 246,000 industrial and commercial buildings were wholly or partly wrecked; an additional 32,000 public structures were ruined. All the raw material stocks were seized by the Germans and 6,640,000 acres of land were made unfit for cultivation.

The transportation system, the lifeblood of the nation's economy, was all but crippled. About half the locomotives and one-third of the merchant marine were destroyed or seized. Around three-fourths of the harbor facilities and freight yards were in ruins. Railroad tracks and bridges were wrecked throughout France, resulting in 14,000 locomotives seized, damaged, or destroyed; 325,000 passenger and freight cars destroyed; 2,000 miles of railway tracks wrecked; 780,000 motor vehicles destroyed; 6,800 railway and road bridges blown up; and 1,500,000 tons of shipping lost.

Not counting human lives, the total cost of the physical destruction has been estimated, at 1938 prices, at 1,000 billion francs, or 28 billion dollars.

At the Liberation, therefore, the French faced a monumental task of reconstruction. The very clearing away of the wreckage required immense labor and effort. One example will illustrate the problem. Before France could begin rebuilding, she had to remove a vast number of land mines from fields, homes, and streets in nearly every department, for the whole country had been a battlefield. In some departments, nearly one million mines had to be cleared. It took a few years to remove the mines, as the following table shows:

AREAS COMPLETELY CLEARED, JUNE 1, 1946

Departments	Number of Mines	Hectares*
Oise	20,542	20
Vendée	184,291	641
Basses-Pyrénées	82,051	1,068
Pyrénées-Orientales	237,323	6,326
Herault	997,590	15,461
Basses-Alpes	8,851	7,475
Hautes-Alpes	2,807	4,391
Seine-et-Marne	17,869	35

*A hectare is 2.471 acres.

AREAS PARTLY CLEARED

Departments	Number of Mines	Hectares*	Percentage of Area
Aisnes	9,695	23	99%
Charente	357,867	2,560	87
Eure	10,012	53	56
Ille-et-Vilaine	109,226	1,713	96
Landes	195,773	1,973	93
Aude	265,420	4,397	99
Bouches-du-Rhône	674,490	55,302	92
Var	373,889	9,075	92

*A hectare is 2.471 acres.

Immediately after the Liberation, the French began the backbreaking task of rebuilding the country. A number of steps had to be taken simultaneously, but the first and important one was the restoration of the transportation network. This was done in record time, despite the shortage of rolling stock and the obsolescence of equipment. Other steps were to provide power, particularly coal and electricity, and to restore production, largely in the heavy industry.

By 1948 the French railroads (S.N.C.F.) succeeded in attaining a 50 percent increase over the 1939 traffic, with equipment still decidedly inferior to that of the prewar period. At the same time, it must be admitted, passenger comfort has sharply declined. The average number of passengers per train has risen from 80 in 1928 to 220 in 1948. The merchant fleet, particularly freighters and tankers, was fully re-created by 1949.

The French achieved a veritable miracle of reconstruction. By 1946, within two years after the Liberation, the volume of production had risen to about 90 percent of prewar levels. Today many industries are producing far more than they did before 1938, and all homemade consumers' articles are available and as plentiful as before the war.

In 1946 the French took a remarkable economic step. They set up a Planning Commission to modernize and equip the country. The Commissariat général du Plan de Modernisation et d'Équipement, headed by Jean Monnet, adopted a four-year program to modernize the obsolete plant and to raise the levels of production in six major sectors of the French economy. Agricultural machinery output was to be raised by 27 percent over 1938, building materials 40 percent, mining 13 percent, transportation 57 percent, and steel 46 percent. Exports and imports, as well as loans, were also to be regulated and adjusted under the Plan. Altogether, it envisioned an over-all increase in national production of 30 percent above 1938.

The total cost of investment provided for in the Plan was about 18,900,000,000 dollars. Most of the money, about 84 percent, was to be provided by the French themselves; the rest was to come from loans,

mainly American. The Plan also required heavy-imports machinery, raw
materials, and, especially, coal and oil. Up through the year 1949 the
United States continued to be France's main single source of supplies.
In 1949 nearly one-fourth (24 percent) of all imports into France came
from the United States.

The Monnet Plan aimed to reduce sharply this dependence on imports.
It was designed to give France and her overseas territories great industrial strength and a measure of economic independence. For France had
always been a heavy importer of certain essential materials, and hence
in a dependent position. Before the war, for example, France imported:
coal 35 percent; paper pulp 54 percent; fats 60 percent; lead 65 percent;
wool 87 percent; cotton 96 percent; copper, zinc, and tin 98 percent.

More than one thousand specialists worked out the Monnet Plan. They
were drawn from industry, government, schools, and trade unions. The
latter, in particular, were co-operative. The C. G. T. went so far as to
agree to a forty-eight-hour work week, in place of the legal forty hours,
and to do all in its power to promote the objectives of the great Plan.

On November 27, 1946, Jean Monnet made the Plan public. He stated
that by 1950 France would be stronger economically than she had ever
been before in her history.

GOALS OF THE MONNET PLAN

Basic Industries and Transport, 1947—50

Industries	Units	1938	1950
Coal mining	Millions of tons	47.6	65
Electricity	Billions kw. hrs.	20.7	37*
Hydroelectric power	Billions kw. hrs.	11.6	20.5**
Iron and steel	Millions of tons	6.2	11
Cast iron	Millions of tons	0.7	2.7
Cement	Millions of tons	4.1	18.5
Agricultural machinery	Thousands	2.7	16
Highway transport†	Thousands of tons carrying capacity	1,100	1,470˘

*39.5 in 1951
**23 in 1951.
†Vehicles of two tons or more.

The Monnet Plan has more than fulfilled expectations in several areas.
Recovery and reconstruction have been continuing almost uninterruptedly
throughout the whole economy. By the first quarter of 1948 the production
of automobiles had gone up 4.7 percent over 1938, steel 17 percent, cement
30 percent, electricity 40 percent. Production continues to rise steadily.
By 1950 total industrial production was around one-third higher than in
1938. Steel, of which nearly 8 million tons were produced in 1929, is

expected to reach the 12-million mark in 1953. Electricity, although it is up more than one-third over 1938, is still insufficient to meet the growing need. New hydroelectric dams and power plants are now in process of construction.

France's automobile industry is an example of her growing economic strength. This is one of the small number of large-scale, mass-producing industries. The nationalized Renault motor works now produces approximately 315 vehicles daily. In the first ten months of 1949 the automobile industry totaled 230,594 vehicles, of which 147,366 were cars.[17] The monthly average has been about 18,000, as against some 15,000 in 1938. In 1948 France exported more than half (57 percent) of the passenger cars and 14 percent of the commercial vehicles to European countries and the Americas, earning a total of 144 million dollars. In that year the United States alone bought 3,200 Renault cars.

The production of tractors has been especially marked. France produces now about 22,000 tractors a year, about thirteen times more than the 1,700 in 1938. Tractor production is concentrated in a few plants. Renault produces 40 percent of the total, and three other firms another 35 percent. There has also been a striking increase in the production of other farm machinery, especially for the dairy industry, which in the long run, should enable France to reduce the costs of agricultural produce. France still has many difficult social and economic problems to solve, but one thing is clear— on the industrial front she is now doing better than in the pre-World War II period.

8. Nationalization

An important aspect of the French economy is the nationalization of certain basic industries and utilities. The whole problem of nationalized industries is still a subject of intense dispute, and even doubt, for in some ways it has led France to a kind of suspended economic limbo. There is not enough nationalization to transform France into a full socialist state, and too much to permit it to be a genuine capitalist one. (See also Chapter II, Section 3.) The French public itself, moreover, does not seem to know where it stands in this respect or what it wants. This is not just a simple division of opinion between those who are for and those who are against nationalization. It is plainly a question of the absence of clarity of purpose. There is no clearly defined tendency in any direction.

Nobody seems to know for sure whether nationalized enterprises benefit the economy or not, whether they are inefficiently administered or not. There is no certainty as to whether they should be extended or reduced. Enemies of nationalization charge the system with wastefulness and political domination. Friends worry, because they suspect the accusations are true. Thus the first public policy statement of André Marie, when he became Premier in July 1948, dealt with nationalization. He said: "We want nationalized enterprises to become a source of pride for France and to cease being a source of anxiety."

There are a number of reasons, political, economic, and moral, for the nationalization program. The first steps were taken in 1936, by the Popular Front government, under pressure of the Socialist and Communist coalition. The government then nationalized, first, the Bank of France, the munitions and aviation industries, and the railroads. The Bank of France was nationalized because it had long been too powerful for the democracy; indeed, not infrequently it was instrumental in the overthrow of cabinets and, though a private corporation, it had the right to issue money. Nationalization of the armaments and aviation industries was defended on the ground that, at a time of world crisis when global conflict was threatening, it was morally wrong to allow private profit from the manufacture of the instruments of war. An additional reason given was the need to centralize and supervise war production on a planned basis. Finally, the railroads were nationalized because they were paying their stockholders, not from earned profits but from the common fund, which meant that the national treasury was supporting private individuals.

The railways were nationalized in an unusual way. The Minister of Public Works and the representatives of the railroad companies made an agreement whereby the latter turned over to the S. N. C. F. (Société Nationale des Chemins de Fer Français, or National Society of French Railroads) their franchises, but retained title to the property. In return for the franchises, the companies received from the S. N. C. F. "A" stocks to be divided among the shareholders in 1956. The government itself kept a majority of the stock and majority control in the Board of Directors, as well as the Administrative Committee. In the two latter bodies, the president and vice-president must be chosen from representatives of the government; and the Minister of Public Works must approve all nominations to important positions on the railroads. Thus, for all practical purposes the government controls the railways.

After the Liberation there was a climate of opinion favoring further nationalization. For one thing, the general tendency in France and, indeed, in Europe as a whole was in the direction of more and more intervention on the part of the state in the social and economic affairs of the country. For another, there was a desire to free the government from the "money power" of the so-called "Two Hundred Families," who had unquestionably wielded immense influence under the Third Republic.

Finally, there was a grievance against the big capitalists. Many of them— Renault, for example— had been either Nazi collaborationists during the war and occupation or outright Fascists. Heavy industry, notably steel, had given Hitler support in the 'thirties. The Comité de Forges helped in the rearmament of Germany not only by starving France's own vitally needed steel industry but also by selling Hitler French-produced ore. In 1936 France exported to Germany 8 million tons of ore, and continued to do so— at the rate of 800,000 a month in the last year— until the very outbreak of World War II. When the war was over, there prevailed, therefore, a bitter feeling against the industrialists, who had shown that their primary love was not for France but for francs.

These were some of the reasons why, after the Liberation, the dominant political parties favored nationalization of the basic industries and utilities. Among the most important enterprises that were nationalized were: coal (Charbonnages de France), electricity (Électricité de France), gas (Gaz de France), insurance companies, banks, and certain industries that had belonged to collaborationists, such as the Renault motor works. The government did not confiscate those properties but paid for them with bonds redeemable in fifty years. The nominal value of the bonds was based on the average price of the stocks over a period specified in each case by the law. Interest rates were set according to the enterprise involved. In the case of banks and insurance companies, the law required that the interest could not be lower than the dividend rate prevailing in the fiscal year 1944. For the banks the rate could not be higher and for the insurance companies lower than 3 percent.

The nationalized industries are managed by administrative councils, consisting of representatives of consumers, workers, employees, and the State. In practice, however, the government exercises control, particularly since it has power over wages, prices, and investments. The nationalized sector may, therefore, be described as Statism rather than Socialism.

Nationalized enterprises have suffered from the usual ills of French society— excessive individualism, inefficiency, bureaucratization, and political meddling. In general, public opinion has been critical. Since it would not be politically expedient to abolish the nationalized industries, it is necessary to reform them. One proposed reform is to decentralize the whole nationalized sector and elect workmen administrators by secret ballot.

Whether unavoidably or not, the nationalized businesses have been losing money. In 1948 the coal mines lost 20 billion francs, the electric utilities 6 billion, the railways 28 billion, and Air France 1 billion. The total deficit was 55 billion francs, or around 172 million dollars. In 1949 the railways had a deficit of 21 billion francs.

The way the situation is now it seems fairly certain that, for the time being at least, there will be no further extension of nationalization. It is also doubtful whether the nationalized enterprises will ever be restored to private ownership. A recent public opinion poll showed 54 percent as believing that there has been too much nationalization, 14 percent thought not enough, and 7 percent said it was exactly comme il faut. One fourth, mostly women and farmers, expressed no opinion.

The chances are probably that the nationalized industries and public utilities will remain public property, but that under pressure and criticism they will improve in service and efficiency. If France's private economy should acquire great health and vigor, it would undoubtedly serve as a stimulant and corrective on the nationalized sector.

9. Agriculture and Food

Before the war the rich soil of France was sufficient to provide the

nation with virtually everything needed to eat and drink well. Farming
was essentially small-scale and individualistic, with the exception of viti-
culture, where big organizations and co-operatives are not uncommon.
There was little mechanization. Power on the farms was supplied by the
muscle of man and beast. Farming was, therefore, inefficient by modern
standards. In the period of 1933−37, for example, the average yield of
wheat per hectare was 15 quintals in France as against 23 in Germany.
The war caused immense destruction of farmhouses, livestock, equipment, and seeds; and during a large part of that period France went
hungry. After the Liberation American aid and then the Marshall Plan
gave a powerful boost to French agriculture and, ultimately, to the food
supply. "Le Plan Marshall," Minister of Agriculture Pflimlin told a group
of us on June 14, 1949, at St. Lo on the occasion of the delivery of a
number of American tractors, "played a decisive role in French recovery."
More and more French farmers are using mechanical aid on the land.
(See also Chapter IV, Section 7.) There has been, in consequence, a tre-
mendous improvement in the food situation in record time. Early in 1949
nearly all food rationing— the bane and misery of ten years— was abolished
and today the French people eat about as well as they did before the war,
although prices are still too high. It took only about four years, since the
Liberation, to achieve levels of near-normalcy in food production.

PRODUCTION OF SOME FOODSTUFFS
(In round figures)

	1938	1948
Meat	1,700,000 tons	1,600,000 tons
Wine	58,900,000 hectoliters	47,000,000 hectoliters
Wheat	80,000,000 quintals	74,000,000 quintals
Milk	138,000,000 hectoliters	120,000,000 hectoliters
Potatoes	170,000,000 quintals	166,000,000 quintals
Sugar	860,000 tons	850,000 tons

Unfortunately for the French people as a whole, particularly the wage
earners, prices of agricultural products and foodstuffs did not go down
with the increase in production. As a matter of fact, wages have nowhere
kept pace with the cost of food, and this has aggravated the political situation, created bitterness among city people, and has led to one cabinet
crisis after another. Food costs today are actually from ten to twenty-two
times higher than in 1938. Cereals cost over twelve times as much as they
did in 1938, and meats and lards about twenty-three times as much. The
over-all wholesale index of food prices is about nineteen times higher
than in 1938.

It must be repeated that wages and salries have not kept up anywhere
with the cost of food, or other needs. Most of the French people, therefore,
are in real trouble. The majority spend the bulk of their earnings on food,

which is abundant, and have little left for other necessities or services. Until food prices and earnings will have reached a common level, France will be in a state of unhappiness and crisis.

10. Trade Unions

Unlike the prewar period, organized labor is a strong force in France today. Joining a trade union is no longer an act of faith or defiance, as it used to be before 1938, but a necessity of employment. Since 1946 the unions choose shop stewards in every plant and participate in management councils. Plant Committees, which submit suggestions to management, are a widespread institution in French industry. The trade unions have a good deal to say in regard to working conditions, methods, promotions, welfare, and so forth. This is especially true in the nationalized industries.

Before the war there were about 4 million trade union members in France. Soon after the Liberation this number had increased to more than 6 million. But in 1946 there took place a great split in the labor movement. A large body of workers broke away from the central trade union body, the Confédération générale du Travail (C. G. T.), because of the latter's domination by the Communists, and formed its own organization, the Force Ouvrière (F. O.). In addition, there is the Confédération française des Travailleurs Chrétiens (C. F. T. C.), which was organized in 1919 on a Catholic, as opposed to Marxist, basis.

These three main labor bodies have been making wild claims about the size of their membership. The Communist C. G. T. claims no fewer than 4 million members; the largely Socialist F. O. says it has 1. 5 million members; and the Catholic C. F. T. C. , 900, 000. Objective figures support none of these claims.

Studies made on the basis of local plants and dues cards show that the C. G. T. probably has around 2, 316, 000 members, the F. O. about 350, 000, and the C. F. T. C. in the neighborhood of 400, 000. Even so, the Communist-dominated C. G. T. has over three times more members than both its chief rivals combined. Communist trade union strength is concentrated among agricultural and industrial laborers, especially miners; while the Socialist and Catholic unions have mostly, although not exclusively, professional and white-collar employees.

In addition to the three big unions, there are a number of small ones. Among them may be mentioned the Comité général du Syndicalisme Indépendant (C. G. S. I.), which probably has around 100, 000 members; the Fédération des Syndicats Autonomes (F. S. A.), which has perhaps 6, 000 members among the metalworkers; and the Confédération nationale du Travail (C. N. T.), with only a few thousand members in Paris and some provincial cities.

It is not without significance that these so-called "Isolés, " or Independents, have already outstripped the Socialist unions, at least in influence and possibly in numbers. This can be seen in the Plant Committees.

At present, of the 3,103 such Committees, the Independents are represented in 740 (24 percent), the Socialist F. O. in 353 (11 percent), the Catholic C. F. T. C. in 551 (17.5 percent), and the Communist C. G. T. in 1,459 (47.5 percent).

Recently, the whole trade union movement has been in the doldrums. Workers have been generally apathetic, especially since the insurrectionary strikes of 1947. But the Communist C. G. T. still maintains a powerful hold over the largest section of France's organized workers.

V. FOREIGN POLICY

1. The Great Defeat of 1940 and Its Consequences

I*

In any consideration of France's relations with the outside world, two observations must be made at the outset: first, that she has ceased to be a major power; second, that she is keenly aware of it.

The plight of France is, of course, not confined to that country alone; it applies equally to all of Europe outside the Soviet Union. But France's awareness of her limited strength has a quality all its own, and is a factor in the total picture. One may say that the consciousness of being feeble adds to the feebleness. As a French newspaperman put it: "The difference between us and the British is that we are both weak, but we know it."

The visible decline of French power was sharp and painful. It occurred only recently—in the fateful June of 1940. And its painfulness has not yet worn off, for a great nation finds it hard to live comfortably with the thought that power has slipped from its hands. By power, of course, I mean control over policy-making decisions. In the vital matter of national security the French no longer have this power. For better or for worse, ultimate decisions affecting the international position of France, and perhaps her very life, are made not by Frenchmen in Paris but by Americans in Washington.

This amounts to a veritable revolution in international affairs. A century and a half ago France was the master of Europe. A century ago she was its most powerful state. A decade ago she was one of the half dozen major powers in the world. Today she cannot even hope to defend her own frontiers.

The extent of the decline of France's power and prestige can be measured by what has happened to French as the language of international discourse. For nearly two and a half centuries French was the language of diplomats— the language in which international instruments were framed. The great international treaties—Rastadt in 1714, Paris in 1763, Vienna in 1814, Berlin in 1878, to mention but a few—were negotiated and drawn up in French. One recalls that at the Congress of Berlin in 1878 when Disraeli wanted to speak English, Bismarck insisted that he use French. Then came 1919 and 1945, two "victories" from which the French have not yet recovered. At Versailles, Wilson and Lloyd George knew little French, while Clemenceau spoke English; consequently the speech of the Anglo-Americans replaced the French language as an instrument of diplomacy, for the first time in generations. But the final mortification came at the San Francisco Conference of the United Nations in 1945, where only three official languages were originally provided for — English, Russian, and Spanish. French was ignored. It was not until Foreign Minister Bidault made a moving speech on behalf of his country's distinguished language

---

*A portion of Section I reprinted by permission from Social Research, Vol. XVI, No. 4 (December 1949).

that French was restored to a position at the international conference table. The external diminution of power and prestige has its reflection in the internal situation. Here, again, we must go back to 1940 to understand the France of today. The depth and extent of the tragedy of 1940 can hardly be overemphasized. For 1940 was not just another military defeat; France, after all, had been defeated before, in 1815 and 1870 for example, without lasting damage. But 1940 was an entirely different kind of disaster. It was smashing defeat, plus humiliation, plus occupation, plus ruinous pillage and destruction, wholly unrelieved. France, in her swift collapse, did not even have the moral satisfaction of having fought heroically in self-defense. The terrible truth is that, with a few rare heroic exceptions, the great French armies simply disintegrated under the first blows of the Nazis.

To the French people the defeat came with a horrifying suddenness and completeness that left them dazed. The one thing Frenchmen had had confidence in was their army. For centuries this had been their security. France's history is, indeed, full of famous generals and of glorious deeds on a thousand battlefields. From the days, in 1106, when Guibert de Nogent wrote his _Gesta Dei per Francos_, a proud account of French heroism in the First Crusade, to 1934, when Charles de Gaulle wrote his _Vers l'armée de métier_, a brilliant analysis of modern warfare (unheeded, alas, by France's General Staff), the French people had had reason to trust the brains and leadership of their top military men. Whatever its faults, the army was the shield of the Republic, the defender of "liberty, fraternity, and equality"—values which themselves had been won in the blood of numerous battles.

The events of 1940 destroyed all this in one crushing blow. France's "Strange Defeat"[18] in 1940 was one of those events that "shook the world." Its swiftness and completeness amazed even the Germans. But the mere fact of the defeat is perhaps less important than the factors that caused it and the reactions that followed it.

II*

A brief historic recapitulation of the war is in order. On September 1, 1939, the Germans invaded Poland, which fell within four weeks. On September 3 France and Great Britain declared war on Germany. But nothing much happened immediately on the Western front. Until the spring of 1940 there were merely feints, skirmishes, and alerts. This was the period that came to be known as "la drôle de guerre"— the Phoney War.

Sitting behind their Maginot Line, the French were confident. On the face of it, they had every reason to be. One of their greatest generals, Maxime Weygand, had assured them publicly in a speech which he delivered at Lille on July 5, 1939:

---

*Sections II–VII reprinted by permission from _World Politics_, April 1950, pp. 307–37.

You ask my opinion of the French army and I will tell you frankly and in all truth.. .. . I believe the French army has a greater value than at any other time in its history: it possesses matériel of first quality, fortifications of the first order, an excellent morale and a remarkable High Command. No one among us desires war, but I affirm that if we are forced to win a new victory, we will win it.

France's military assets were, indeed, seemingly great and a good part of the non-French world shared this confidence in her armed strength. France's navy, under Admiral Darlan, was the fourth most powerful in the world, consisting of 175 warships.[19] The army, about 1 million strong at the front and perhaps 4 million in reserve, had been expensively maintained[20] and was believed to be well trained and expertly led. It lived on the victorious reputation of 1918, and even the idea of total war was not alien to its tradition, for were not the French the first to organize it?[21]

The generals also enjoyed great renown. Chief of Staff Gamelin, for example, had collaborated in the victory of the Marne—a victory immortalized in the famous message from Foch to Joffre: "My right is rolled up; my left is driven back; my center is smashed. I have ordered an advance from all directions." That kind of offensive spirit was supposed to be typical of French arms.

If the French army was not as well equipped as was the Wehrmacht, it was told that it did not really matter, since clearly the individual esprit of the Frenchman was superior to the collective obedience of the German.[22] Above all, the French had morale, and that, the troops were assured, was bound to win in the end. The Règlement d'Infanterie de l'Armée française explained it thus:

> The number and training of the combatants, the power and abundance of the weapons, are not all that count in war. Combat is in the last resort a battle of morale. Whatever may be the material forces employed by one side or the other, they never succeed in the total destruction of the adversary. Among the survivors it is the moral forces that decide victory. The vanquished party is not the one that suffers the most losses in men and matériel, but the one whose morale is the first to bend.

On May 10, 1940, the German blitz struck at the Low Countries; on the 14th the Netherlands Army capitulated. On May 12 the Panzer divisions cut across the Meuse at Sedan, inundated the Belgian plain, turned the French Ninth Army, and raced to the English Channel. Boulogne fell on May 23, Calais on the 25th; two days later, King Leopold, with his army of half a million,[23] surrendered unconditionally and the Allied forces, particularly the British, began their memorable evacuation at Dunkirk, which was completed by June 3.[24]

Having conquered the Low Countries, the Germans cut across the

Somme, flanked the Maginot Line and rushed, virtually unchecked, toward
Normandy and Paris. They took Rouen on the 9th, Villers-Cotterets on the
10th. General Weygand, appointed Commander-in-Chief after the fall of
Holland, was overwhelmed by a sense of defeatism. "Les Allemands,"
he repeated to his staff, "passeront où et quand ils voudront." On June
10 the government quit Paris; on the 12th Weygand ordered a general retreat, and the evacuation of the Maginot Line. 25 Each corps commander
was left to his own resources. 26 On June 14 the Germans entered Paris
and, with the French armies in retreat and in chaos, that was the end.

At ten o'clock on the night of June 16, the French cabinet in Bordeaux,
now infiltrated by defeatists, capitulards, and perhaps outright traitors,
voted thirteen to ten to ask for an armistice. Premier Reynaud resigned
and, with other patriots, soon escaped;27 General Pétain became the
head of the government, assisted by men like Laval, Darlan, and the no-
torious Ybarnegaray, who, when Winston Churchill pleaded for continued
resistance and a union with Britain, cried: "We do not want to become a
British dominion." At noon of June 17, less than five weeks after the
German blitz started, Pétain told the French people to stop fighting. In a
radio address he said: "It is with a heavy heart that I tell you that it is
necessary to cease the combat."28

The armistice was signed on June 25, President of the Republic Lebrun
was forced to resign, and helpless France was carved up between the
German conquerors who kept the northern half, and the French Fascists
and collaborationists who preserved the southern portion. From 1,500,000
to 1,900,000 French soldiers were taken prisoner by the Germans, which
constituted perhaps the largest military disaster in history.

Thus the German lightning struck France and brought her crashing to
the ground. It took the Germans a mere forty days of military operations—
at a minimum cost to themselves29— to annihilate the proudest army in
Europe, to make a mockery of the most elaborate fortifications, to reduce
to nullity the most pretentious General Staff. In forty days France, the
world's second largest empire and for centuries one of the masters of
Europe, ceased to exist as a power. It was all so swift and overwhelming
that the French people were left dazed, crushed in spirit, tearful and un-
believing. They did not know what hit them, and to this day it is not certain
that they know.

Who was responsible for the national catastrophe? If blame for the
debacle is to be allocated, one cannot absolve the whole people. Obviously
everybody was to a certain extent morally responsible: the Left for its
pacifism, the Right for its defeatism, the rest of the nation for its je m'en
foutisme. 30 But moral judgments apart, one discerns three main causes
behind France's disaster. They can be described as the three M's—Men,
Materials, and Mind. In other words, the defeat was caused by bad leadership, especially military; by insufficient matériel, poorly organized; and
by a low state of public opinion, including that of the troops.

III

Men. — It is now universally known that the French High Command was pitifully, one might say totally, inept. Coming from a society that was, in most fields, virtually a gerontocracy, the top military men were old in 1940 — Gamelin, for example, was 61, Weygand 73, Pétain 84. They lived in the past and possessed, no doubt, fine nineteenth-century minds. Their military training and experience made them feel at home in cavalry and horse-drawn cannon; modern machines, the co-ordination of swift and mechanized weapons with striking manpower was beyond their conception. Theirs was a strategy of passivity, dominated by "le fétichisme de la ligne Maginot. "[31] The immediate responsibility for the debacle must, thus, be placed squarely on the French High Command with its rigidity and lack of imagination. [32] As General Joffre once remarked: "I do not know whether it was I who won the battle of the Marne, but one thing I do know well— if it had been lost, it would have been by me. "

An additional factor was pro-Fascist sympathy on the part of many of France's top figures, in the army, navy, and government. The blunt truth is that a number of influential Frenchmen in key positions hated the Republic, and others turned out to be downright traitors. At best, the leading generals were politically conservative and limited in outlook, like General Giraud, [33] or inclined to a bumbling kind of patriarchal fascism like General Pétain. [34] At worst, they were men like Generals Dentz and Bridoux, whom French courts later condemned to death. In the army, the spirit that had led to the Dreyfus case was still alive. Indeed, Weygand, an antirepublican, had, as a young captain, contributed ten francs for a monument to Colonel Henry, [35] a French General Staff officer whose forged letter had helped to condemn Dreyfus. [36] As Generalissimo in 1940, Weygand was a defeatist from the moment he took over command; [37] his political convictions being what they were, he could hardly have been expected to put his heart into the war against the Nazi-Fascists. He helped further to depress the spirit of the French cabinet, which had fled to the provinces, by repeating the canard that a Communist uprising was about to take place at Paris. Minister of Interior Mandel challenged the statement and, while not calling the General a liar, proved that he was not telling the truth. [38]

A fundamental reason for the behavior of many French leaders was the fear of communism. Right-wing circles were easily persuaded that the real enemy of France was communism and not Hitlerism— a cardinal theme in Nazi propaganda. Their definition of communism included everything on the Left, from anti-Communist Socialists to anti-Socialist liberals. It is not certain that many could or cared to tell the difference between a democratic Socialist and a totalitarian Communist. To the Right, everybody more or less on the Left was a "Red. " The claims of democracy were considered and labeled "Communist. "

The Rightist generals were not alone in their antipathy to democracy. High naval officers were, if anything, more hostile to the democratic Third

Republic, which they despised. A restricted caste recruited from the old families, clerical and reactionary as a rule, they lived in a never-never political world. On top of everything, they hated the British ally, whom they considered a more deadly rival than the Germans whose fleet had never been sufficiently important for rivalry. In spirit they were not at war with Germany but with Britain.[39] One of the few pro-Republican French admirals (in private conversation he insisted he was the only one) told this writer that during the 1936 maneuvers in the Mediterranean he became so fed up with the conversation of his officers about preferring "Hitler to Blum" that he finally ordered them to leave the table.[40]

Among civilians, the number of pro-Germans and sympathizers with Nazi-fascism was, of course, legion. Although it is an exaggeration to say, as did Pierre Cot,[41] that the French bourgeoisie as a whole was converted to fascism, it is certainly true that large numbers of leading figures in government, in industry, and in the professions were in sympathy with the Hitler-Mussolini ideology. Their motivations varied from the careerism (plus hatred of Britain) of a Laval, through the Fascist convictions of a Deat, to the gangsterism of a Darnand.[42]

Whatever their motives, it is certain that numerous Frenchmen were ready to deliver their country to Hitler and, later, to collaborate with the Germans in the transformation of France into a second-rate Fascist dependency. Their eagerness to serve the enslavers of their country sometimes embarrassed the more sensitive Germans, as can be seen in the remarkable diary of Ernst Juenger, the German novelist who served as a staff officer during the occupation in Paris. Juenger comments with dry irony in his diary[43] that no matter what dirty work the Germans needed done, they always found Frenchmen willing to do it for them.

After the Liberation, the French who had fought in the Resistance set up tribunals to try the traitors and collaborationists— exactly as Pétain and his collaborationist generals had done in 1940.[44] There were three kinds of courts: local F.F.I.[45] courts martial; special justice courts to hear cases of collaboration; and the High Court of Justice in Paris for prominent figures. These courts were organized in tacit agreement between the Communists and the Gaullists; each group apparently agreed to defend its class and spare the other's.[46] Thus neither workers nor big industrialists were tried. Nor was a single general shot. Those executed were civilians, mostly intellectuals.[47]

In a period of about five years the various courts rendered verdicts on 129,000 cases of collaboration. Of these, 791 were executed;[48] 38,000 were given prison sentences;[49] and 48,000 were attainted with "national indignity."[50] Any way one looks at it, this is an exceedingly high number for a "Nation of Patriots."[51]

In terms of the personalities judged, the most important of the tribunals was the Haute Cour de Justice, created on November 13, 1944, to try collaborators of high rank. The court sat until the end of June 1949 when it was officially closed. In the course of almost four and a half years of its existence it handed down eighteen death sentences, ten of them in absentia. Of these, only three have been carried out; five, including Pétain, were commuted to life imprisonment; three committed suicide in prison. Thirty were condemned to national degradation and perpetual forced labor; ten were acquitted; three died before trial.

A partial list of the 108 prominent collaborators accused before the High Court is shown in the table on pages 68–69.[52]

All this adds up to a kind of revolution, incomplete and aimless to be sure, but deep-reaching and with incalculable potentialities for further explosion. In terms of larger politics, the defeat of 1940, followed by the repressions of Vichy and succeeded by the severe purges of the Liberation, revealed the extent of national disunity. It showed the depth of disaffection toward the Republic and the existing institutions on the part of important segments of the French population, both on the Right and on the Left. So fragile have been the foundations of national unity— the Third Republic, it will be recalled, was saved in 1875 by the margin of one vote— that the harsh blow of a crisis, instead of consolidating the nation, only splintered it further. Great numbers of Frenchmen have had, as they still have, other loyalties than to fellow Frenchmen or to the Republic (Third or Fourth).[53]

IV

Materials. — Next to the inept generalship and collaborationism as direct factors in the defeat of 1940, there was the question of the inadequacy of military matériel. In the last analysis, of course, the difficulty here may be ascribed to the fact that France is, and has been, an underindustrialized country. Most of France's industry, moreover, was small-scale, insufficiently powered,[54] and, consequently, ill-prepared to produce material and parts in the mass that modern warfare requires. In the matter of steel-producing capacity alone, for instance, the Germans exceeded them at least sixfold. It has been estimated that if France had been properly industrialized and economically organized, she could have equipped and maintained no less than 110 divisions.[55]

But even the inadequate matériel that did exist was not well used, and in certain instances not at all. Here we must touch upon an essential point, that of organization for use. A crated tank in storage is obviously of no value to men in the field; and in the case of France in 1940 much of the materials of war never reached the troops. This was not necessarily sabotage, as has been charged often, but, to use the inelegant but precisely descriptive American Army slang, just plain snafu. The snafu that prevailed in high French circles, military as well as civilian, can be judged from the fact that neither the Prime Minister nor the generals were informed, at the most critical moments, about the planes that the French Army had at its disposal. Worse than that, they could not get the exact information even when they tried.

The French were warned about the Luftwaffe and its preparations.

A PARTIAL LIST OF THE 108 PROMINENT COLLABORATORS
ACCUSED BEFORE THE HIGH COURT

Name	Position	Sentence	Present status
Pétain, Philippe	Chief of State	Death	Commuted to life[1]
Laval, Pierre	Chief of Government	Death	Executed[2]
Darnand, Joseph	Chief of Militia	Death	Executed[3]
Brinon, Fernand de	Secretary of State	Death	Executed
Dentz, General	Resident General in Syria	Death	Died at Fresnes[4]
Dayras, Georges	Secretary General in Ministry of Justice	Death	Commuted to life[5]
de Laborde, Admiral	Commander of Mediterranean fleet	Death	Commuted to life[6]
Benoist-Mechin	Secretary of State	Death	Commuted to life[7]
Deat, Marcel	Minister of Labor	Death	Disappeared[8]
Bonnard, Abel	Minister of Education	Death	In Madrid[9]
Gabolde, Maurice	Keeper of the Seals	Death	In Spain[10]
Bonnefoy, Réné	Secretary General of Information	Death	Disappeared
Rochat, Louis	Secretary General in Foreign Office	Death	In Switzerland[11]
Alibert, Raphael	Keeper of the Seals	Death	Disappeared
Guerard, Jacques	Secretary General of Chief of Government	Death	In Spain[12]
Darquier de Pellepoix	Commissioner of Jewish Questions	Death	In Madrid[13]
Masson, André	Minister of Prisoners	Death	Disappeared
Bridoux, General	Under Secretary of State for Air in War Ministry	Death	Escaped[14]
Esteva, Admiral	Governor General of Tunis	Life	At Clairvaux
Vallat, Xavier	Commissioner of Jewish Questions, later of Information	10 yrs.	At Clairvaux
Chasseigne, François	Secretary of State for Food, later Labor	10 yrs.	At Clairvaux
Marion, Paul	Secretary of State for Information	10 yrs.	At Clairvaux
Chevallier, Jacques	Minister of Education	20 yrs.	Reduced to 4

Name	Position	Sentence	Present status
Abrial, Jean	Admiral	10 yrs.	Reduced to 4
Marquis	Admiral	5 yrs.	Reduced to 4
Baudouin, Paul	Minister of Foreign Affairs	20 yrs.	Reduced to 4
Laure	General		Acquitted
Peyrouton, Marcel	Minister of Interior, then Ambassador		Acquitted[15]
Martin, Oliver			Acquitted

[1]Nov. 15, 1945, Pétain was transferred to the fort on the Ile d'Yeu in the Atlantic.

[2]After taking poison, Laval was executed in Fresnes prison on Oct. 15, 1945.

[3]Executed on Oct. 10, 1945, in the fort of Chatillon; one day later, in the same place, Jean-Herold Paquis, the military commentator on Radio Paris from 1941 to 1944, was also executed.

[4]Condemned to death on Aug. 20, 1945, he was "gracié" to life by General de Gaulle on Oct. 25, but died in Fresnes.

[5]Held at Clairvaux.

[6]It was Admiral de Laborde who scuttled the fleet at Toulon; he is now at Clairvaux.

[7]Now at the Ile de Ré.

[8]Condemned in absentia. Believed either to have found death during his flight in the Alps, or to live in Brazil.

[9]Condemned in absentia. In Madrid he makes a living as a journalist and lecturer.

[10]Condemned in absentia. Lives in poverty in Spain.

[11]Lives as a translator.

[12]Some believe he is head of an insurance company there; others think he is in Argentina.

[13]He may be somewhere in South America now.

[14]Before his trial, he escaped from the Val-de-Grâce to Madrid, where he is now writing his memoirs.

[15]Acquitted on Dec. 22, 1948, largely because of the role he played in the arrest and banishment of Pierre Laval from Vichy. It was also counted in his favor that General Giraud had persuaded General Eisenhower to bring him to North Africa and make him Governor of Algeria. General Eisenhower writes in his Crusade in Europe: "In the search for satisfactory individuals we decided to bring Marcel Peyrouton to Algiers. It was reported to me that Peyrouton was then a virtual exile in Argentina, unable to go back to France because of the enmity of Laval, Hitler's most evil puppet. It was also reported that he had previously established a reputation in North Africa as a skillful colonial administrator. Nevertheless, he had been, for a considerable time, a member of the Vichy Government and was therefore regarded in the democratic world as a Fascist. Bringing Peyrouton to Algeria as Governor was a mistake, even though he was a vast improvement over his soft and vacillating predecessor."

They had shocking evidence of the power and the co-ordinated use of
Goering's bombers and fighters after the Polish campaign. The Prime
Minister and his General Staff knew, in the autumn of 1939, that the Germans disposed of 4,000 warplanes poised for action, 5,000 planes in reserve, and 3,000 training and supply planes. [56] What did the French have,
and how did they prepare to meet this situation?

On February 13, 1940, a few weeks before the German attack on the
Low Countries, Prime Minister Daladier called a conference of his war
chiefs, including Generals Gamelin and Georges and the heads of the Min-
istries of War and Air. General Georges reported that the First French
Armée aérienne, held in preparation for operations in the Northeast, consisted of 936 planes, 288 old ones and 648 recent ones. But, added the
General, of the 648, only 453 were "ready for action," and none was a
bomber— 350 were pursuit planes, and 81 reconnaissance and observation
craft.

General Georges was obviously perturbed at his own revelation. The
Prime Minister pointed out that in 1939 France had produced 2,400 planes
(1,450 of them fighters), and asked: "Où sont ces avions?" Nobody could
tell him.

A few days later, on February 22, Minister of Air Guy la Chambre
sent a note to Daladier challenging General Georges' figures. Instead of
648 modern planes, the note stated, the First Air Army had 703, of which
520 were disponible. It added that there existed also one bombardment
group and three fighter groups in the Southeast.

On the following day the bedeviled Daladier received a report informing
him that in the month of January France produced a total of 326 planes
(sortis d'usine) but only 209 were, in effect, listed as effective (pris en
compte). He could not understand it, and scribbled on the margin: "Qu'on
m'explique la différence!" In three days he was given an explanation by
the National Defense Department of the Cabinet— that when a plane leaves
the factory it has to be tested, and only after it meets the test is it pris
en compte. [57]

The documents show that in the weeks preceding the German blitz, Daladier was worried about aviation. From the Air Ministry, the Air Generals,
and the Chief of Staff he tried to get la vérité about the situation, but all
he obtained was either assurances of false optimism[58] or contradictory
accounts. On March 18 a report reached his desk that, as of January 30,
France possessed a total of 2,449 planes, of which less than half (1,221)
were assigned to the armies at the front. But even then the truth was not
explained to him. He was not informed that of the total available to the
troops, 700 or 800 were pursuit planes, and that of these, one-third were
indisponible, that is, not ready for action. In different words, only 450 to
500 planes were ready to take to the air as fighters. In addition, there were
perhaps 60 bombers and about 150 observation and reconnaisance planes.

This situation remained more or less unchanged at the time when the
Germans struck in their brilliantly combined tank and infantry offensive

whose path was cleared by the massive sweep of the hundreds of <u>Luftwaffe</u> bombers. On May 14, four days after the start of the German blitz, a report was put on Daladier's desk containing the following information about the state of French fighter craft:

		Craft	
Date	No. Pilots	Existing	Available
May 10, a. m.	428	579	429
May 12, 9:00 p. m.	467	518	323

On that day seven German armored divisions, preceded by a <u>Luftwaffe</u> which had absolute control of the skies, crossed the Ardennes without firing a shot. They rolled, unhindered, at night with lights blazing. The French, with their few tardily and hastily (in 1939) organized tanks[59] and no aviation to speak of, stood helplessly by as German armor roared into their country. In the air, the few hundred French planes made pathetic attempts to stem the German avalanche. But all the courage and gallantry of the French pilots were a vain sacrifice.[60] The odds, in numbers and speed, were overwhelmingly against them. They were simply blown out of the skies.[61]

V

<u>Mind.</u> — Perhaps more fatal than the incompetence of the leaders and the shortage of military matériel was the lack of fighting spirit. In 1939–40 France's morale, both civilian and military, had hit bottom. The soul of the nation was corroded by fear and doubt, and upon this state of demoralization Nazi propaganda played unceasingly.

The country was splintered politically and morally. On the extreme Right, the influential Fascist movement, a wing of which was directly connected with the Nazis and another of which was a native product, operated under the slogan, "Why Die for Danzig?" Clever Fascist agitators like Deat and Doriot ridiculed the whole system of alliances so laboriously built up since 1919 and, thereby, helped to undermine the country's foreign policy and its self-confidence. On the extreme Left, the powerful Communist Party, especially after the Russo-German Pact of 1939, poisoned large sections of the working class with the notion that the struggle against Hitler was an "imperialist war." This was remarkably effective propaganda, although for sheer shortsightedness and stark cynicism it has rarely been excelled. Caught between these extremes was the bewildered middle class and peasantry, torn by uncertainty and dubious whether the war against Hitler made any sense. In other words, France had neither war aims nor convictions; she went into battle with heavy heart and no purpose. The general feeling was the weary "<u>Il faut en finir.</u>"

The lack of moral preparation for war reflected itself most acutely in the army. Not only was there no political indoctrination of the troops, but, on the contrary, outright skepticism, defeatism, and antimilitarism.

Partly, this was due to class feeling and resentment of the officers
who were usually of bourgeois or well-to-do peasant origin. They did not
always treat the lower ranks with respect or accord them proper dignity.[62]

Partly, the defeatism of the army was a matter of Communist, as well
as Nazi, propaganda, which was most corrosive among the soldiers who
came from the working class. A man who served in the Foreign Legion in
1939—40, and was later gravely wounded, told this writer that the French
Sergeant who drilled them gave them daily sneering "pep talks" to the
effect that the whole bunch of them must be "really stupid types to volun-
teer to fight for those imperialist cochons." Later when his Foreign
Legion company went into action (their casualties were 90 percent), he
recalled bitterly how the native French troops watched them mockingly
and jeered: "Go to it, gars!" The implication was— Boys, it's your war!

This is not, it goes without saying, a reflection on the courage of the
French. For centuries they had been one of the great warrior peoples,
and they had proven their bravery in thousands of battles in the past.[63]
In 1940, too, there were instances of French soldiers and officers who
fought heroically against crushing odds, who resisted to the bitter end
even after everything was lost, even after the Command had given orders
to retire or surrender. This writer knows of one machine gun unit which,
cut off from its own division and command, continued to retreat and resist
and fire at the advancing Germans from behind every cover until the last
round of ammunition was expended. There were men and officers whose
hearts broke when they were ordered to give up and who burst into tears
of rage and humiliation when the news of the armistice was announced.
The fine old French spirit was by no means dead in 1940. And later, after
1941 and 1942, when the underground was organized, tens of thousands of
Frenchmen knew how to fight and die with a courage that was beyond praise.
The record of the Free French, too, is by no means the least heroic epi-
sode of World War II.[64] For as General Eisenhower observed, when the
French feel they have something to fight for they are "soldiers of the first
order."

But the army as a whole in 1940 was not permeated with fighting spirit,
any more than was the nation. Where morale is absent, individual bravery
becomes merely futile; and morale is the result of pride in belonging, trust
in leadership, and confidence in victory. None of these elements existed
in the French Army of 1940.

Recently there has come to light a story that illuminates, like a sudden
flash in the dark, the state of terror and panic and demoralization of the
French troops in the face of the advancing enemy.

On June 20, 1940, in the hamlet of Tantimont near Germonville (Meurthe-
et-Moselle), elements of the 23d and 153d artillery regiments found themselves encircled by the Germans. For days they had been retreating, destroying much of their matériel as they fell back. Colonel de Peninou of
the 23d had been wounded, and Lieutenant Colonel Charly of the 153d took
over command of the two artillery remnants.

Charly was a superior officer, kindly toward his men and concerned

with their welfare. But on that June 20 he was bitter at the constant re-
treats and determined to fight. His batteries were placed in an orchard
along the highway at the outskirts of the village. The men, lying on the
ground near their field pieces, were worn out and disgusted with everything. They wanted to surrender at all costs, and their officers shared
their mood.

Charly assembled his officers and told them of his determination to
continue fighting. He said that he was aware that "all was lost" but that
they were duty-bound to fight in order "to save honor." His order was:
"Pierce the German lines."

The officers were rebellious. Since all was admittedly lost, they ar-
gued that they did not see any reason for sacrificing themselves and their
men. Colonel Charly was so angry at what he considered cowardice and
lack of military honor that at one point he made a gesture as if to reach
for his pistol. He though the better of it and, instead, threatened some of
his subordinates with court-martial for disobedience. Then, accompanied
by his adjutant Leroux, he walked away toward his command post in the
village.

As the auboutiste Colonel passed by his troops, who knew all about the
fight between him and the officers, a shot was fired from the dark into
his back. Charly dropped dead.

A few minutes later, to the relief of the French, the Germans arrived.
They ordered the Colonel to be buried in the village with military honors
and then they took all the troops prisoner. While men and officers were
being rounded up, a German noncom remarked casually that Charly was
not killed by a German bullet. His troops, he said, had not fired a single
shot that evening.

For eight years the tragic fate of Colonel Charly was enshrouded in
silence. But certain rumors would not die. Finally French Military Intelligence started a hush-hush investigation. Witnesses were found to testify
that the bullet that killed Charly came from the direction of the orchard
where the French artillerists were lounging. By a process of gradual
elimination, the search was narrowed down to one man— the Master Gunner,
Fernand Buret.

They found Buret in his native village of Jaulnes, near Bray-sur-Seine,
where he followed the trade of mason. He was a simple man, father of
two children, a respected citizen in his village. He had spent five years
as prisoner of war in Germany.

Arrested, Buret confessed without hesitation. He did, to be sure, fire
the shot that killed the Colonel, but he did not consider himself either
morally or actually guilty— at least no more guilty and no less than his
companions, his sous-officiers and his officers. Any one of the hundreds
of men could or would have pulled the trigger, he felt. It happened that he
did, but he was merely an instrument. All the men shared his feelings and
opinion. That was why his act, although witnessed by dozens of his companions, was covered by an acquiescent silence.

Thus Master Gunner Buret, with his close-cropped head and ordinary,

honest face stood before the military tribunal at Metz, in April 1949, and
told his story. His voice a little désolé, his manner disarming, his shoulder-
shrugs unemphatic and casual, he said to the judge: "For several days
we have been falling back. Many times we asked why weren't we fighting.
. . . We never once fired our cannon. . . . [On June 20] Some of the officers said to the Colonel: 'If we now fire a single cannon we'll all be
massacred.' He answered' 'The first who refuses to obey, I'll blow his
brains out.' . . . I don't know exactly what happened inside myself. My
sous-officier Penzer gave me an order to go and find a munitions truck
abandoned three or four miles away. . . . Somebody handed me a rifle,
saying: 'Kill him! He's going to have us all massacred!' I fired in the
direction of the Colonel."

The judge: "Did you aim?"

Buret, shrugging: "I don't recall."

The judge: "Did you see the Colonel fall?"

Buret was dubious: "I think I went away in the truck. . . . I am not
sure. . . . Soon we were taken prisoner by a few German cyclists. And
nobody asked me how it went. No, I hadn't ever before fired a musket.
What made me lose my head was listening to certain officers saying that
if we fired our cannon we would all be massacred."

In the court there were some thirty visitors, former companions-in-
arms of Buret. To all of them the death of Charly was welcome. It had
saved their lives. And the tribunal did not in all honesty consider Buret
a murderer. He was the creature of the terrible spiritual disorder that
reigned in France in June 1940; he was but one of millions caught in the
national tragedy. The prosecutor did not even ask the court to impose a
severe punishment on Buret, for if the Master Gunner was guilty, then
so was his whole company, and if his company was, so was the whole army
and its command. The implications of condemning a man in Buret's position were too frightening. In the minds of many he could have been a kind
of tragic hero who did what the group of which he was part felt needed doing. [65]

VI

How did the people react to the collapse? When the shock of the catastrophe began to wear off, individuals started to take stock of the situation.
While opinion concerning the events before and subsequent to 1940 has not
yet crystallized, and perhaps never will, certain tendencies have emerged.
They show a groping, if hesitant,[66] attempt to find out the truth.

The French mind after the defeat has been mirrored in a number of
publications, mostly personal and generally tendentious. Among the most
penetrating is Marcel Bloch's L'Étrange Défaite, written as an eyewitness
account in 1940 and not published until six years later. The observations
of Professor Bloch, an officer in the French Army and a distinguished
historian, have a sharp relevancy. As a primary cause of the debacle he
gives "the incapacity of the High Command." The "mental sclerosis,"

he writes, also affected the lower order of officers, all the way down the line. He discusses the lack of liaison, the miserably organized mobilization, the disorders in the various staffs, the bitter spirit of service rivalry, the poor information system in the army, the inability of the officers to command, the bureaucratic conflicts among the officers, the low morale of the troops, and the general demoralization of the nation. The impression created by Bloch is that, even before the Germans fired a shot, France— long misruled by a gouvernement de vieillards— was beaten. [67]

Another thoughtful observer is ex-Ambassador Albert Kammerer who, in 1940, published the clandestine Le Crime de l'Armistice and later a voluminous Vérité sur l'Armistice. His thesis is that in 1940 it was not necessary for France to lay down her arms. A more psychological approach is that of Max Beer who, in La Guerre n'a pas eu lieu, [68] develops the point that French public opinion, lulled by pacifism, was not ready for war. There was also the false sense of security from the existence of the Maginot Line. When the news of the armistice was announced, he writes, "everybody was stupefied" and people began to look for scapegoats. [69] Similarly, Jacques de Launay, in Le Monde en Guerre, [70] seeks the causes of the defeat in the spirit of men: the antimilitarist feeling of French women (in which connection he discusses the influence of Reynaud's friend, Countess Hélène de Portes); the weakness in combat; the outmoded ideas of the General Staff; and the errors of Gamelin's defensive strategy. [71]

The Rightists blame everybody but themselves. Pierre Taittinger, a Paris deputy and member of the Chamber's Army Committee, in his Ce que le pays doit savoir, [72] argues that responsibility for the catastrophe rests with the military chiefs, the politicians, the ministers ("old door-mats"), the Communistic trade-unions, the diplomatic service, and the President of the Republic. [73] Similar arguments are mashaled by the anonymous GYR, in Avant, Pendant, Après le Désastre, [74] where just about everybody, but particularly the politicians from 1919 to 1939, is charged with guilt. Next to the politicians, according to GYR, were the "political scourges"— Jews and Freemasons. This line of thought is pursued in another collaborationist book, that of the deputy Jean Montigny, Toute la Vérité sur un Mois Dramatique de notre Histoire, citing speeches and arguments from Pétain and Laval and others wherein the whole French democratic system is burdened with the responsibility for the defeat. [75]

There is also the Catholic argument. This consists to a great extent of attacks on Marxist materialism with its emphasis on luxury and denial of human dignity and morality. France, according to Catholic thinking, was enfeebled by materialism and in a crisis did not have enough spirit to resist. Hence the Church rallied to Pétain who preached "spiritual" values, such as Honor, Home and Family. [76]

Anti-Fascist circles follow the line of their particular grouping. The Socialists are curiously defensive and feeble in their thinking about 1940 and after. In essence, they insist that Blum is a nice fellow and Pétain is not. [77] The Communists are more vigorous. Theirs is the usual argument

that the capitalists and their assistants, the Socialist politicians, brought
France to disaster. [78] Patriotic Resistants, like Robert Aron and Maurice
Schumann, stress psychological causes. Aron discusses the prevailing
antis in 1940— antimilitarism, anti-Semitism, and anticlericalism— and
points out that the whole nation had, in effect, morally abdicated. [79]

VII

The armistice and defeat brought out a bewildering variety of reactions
among individuals. They are glimpses into national tragedy.

A Foreign Legion officer: "The message of Marshal Pétain announcing
the demand for an armistice fell among us with the effect of a bomb. We
refused to believe it. "[80]

A general already in captivity: "Sadness and consternation on all our
faces. . . . A sentiment of infinite distress. "[81]

A colonel in command of a fortified sector at Haguenau: "We will not
lay down our arms. . . . Let us sing the Marseillaise. "[82]

A Paris surgeon: "I cannot bear it, " and committed suicide. [83]

A sergeant: "We were without news of our families, ignorant of what
was happening to them, tormented by the fear of the worst. "[84]

A man who later became a Resistant: "Some burst into tears, others
sighed with relief. "[85]

François Mauriac, of the French Academy, replying to the question
as to the principal causes of France's debility: "The blood-letting of 1914–
18, the pro-German and anti-French policy of the British after 1918, the
withdrawal of the United States from the League of Nations, and the defeat
of Briand's policy in regard to Germany. "[86]

Madame Leo Lagrange, replying to the same question: "In 1939 fascism
existed inside as well as outside France. That was the main cause, to
which must be added the exhaustion from World War I and the uncertainty
of our foreign policy. "[87]

A Communist worker: "I never hated Germany or the Germans. My
first reaction upon the announcement of the armistice was fear. Everybody
around me was afraid. In the shop where I worked we all agreed there was
no reason to continue the war. Did the troops fight well? Don't make me
laugh, Comrade! What did they have to fight for?"[88]

A librarian, veteran of World Wars I and II: "I never hated the Germans.
Our fighting value? Zero. All the soldiers I was with had only one care—
to escape danger. We all asked: What are we waiting for? Why don't they
conclude an armistice? When the armistice was announced, I remember
I was in a church at Clamecy, and one of our companions, a Communist,

said: 'The capitalist war is over, now we must hold out our hands and re-
join our German comrades.' In the prisoner of war camp where I was nobody ever talked about the armistice or the defeat.''[89]

A Paris lawyer, of Algerian-Jewish descent: "Frankly, I did not hate
the Germans; even my reading of Mein Kampf didn't change my opinion.
I suspended judgment. At the moment of the armistice, the troops in my
unit were totally demoralized, although personally I was ready to fight to
the last drop of blood. Maybe that was because I had no family to worry
about. When the armistice came I had no particular emotion one way or
another. You ask who was responsible for it all? I think it was the extreme
Right and the extreme Left, as well as the regime of ministerial irresponsibility of the Third Republic."

A government official, who had taught history in a Normandy college:
"My interest in regard to Germany related to literature and music. I
read Goethe, and also Rosenberg. But as a Catholic, I was hostile both to
Hitlerism and war. Only after the Austrian Anschluss did I become anti-
German. When the armistice was announced, my first reaction was one of
helplessness. But I was not critical. Being a Cartesian, I suspended judgment, assuming that the French could not do otherwise than they did. Who
is responsible for it all? I think that there exists such a thing as individual
responsibility, but one must always keep in mind that to a certain degree
everybody is. I believe that every Frenchman ought to examine his conscience."

A college teacher, describing himself as a Left-wing Socialist: "An
anti-Fascist, I also believed in the possibility of international understanding. When the war broke out in 1939 I had the premonition that we would
lose it. So the defeat did not come as a surprise; I thought it a historic
necessity. Who was responsible? Why, the whole nation. The French had a
regime that represented them. The only thing that annoyed me when the
armistice was announced was the fact that it was unconditional; that I considered treason. But I must say that I never thought the General Staff had
betrayed us. The High Command made mistakes. As for the causes of
France's debility, one of them may be alcoholism; another, the inadapta-
bility of the government. But the whole historic process was such that one
cannot consider anybody in particular guilty. But these are questions which
should be debated, and I must admit that we French lack the spirit of self-
criticism."

A retired policeman, Catholic and pacifist: "I always said to myself:
Why make war? I was always against it. I tell you frankly if my son weren't
dead, and if war came, I wouldn't let him join. And I'm no Communist.
No, the French didn't fight in 1940, but they did later, when they had something to fight for. Responsibility for the defeat? The politicians! The people
had nothing to do with it. Sure, they voted, but they had no say in the government. I was in Paris when the radio said they were going to fight for

the city; so I took my family and moved away 500 kilometers. When the armistice was declared, I tell you truly I sighed with relief. So did most people."

2. Communism

An understanding of France's foreign policy in general and European union in particular requires a discussion of two salient problems. One is communism; the other, relations with Germany.

First, it should be kept in mind that, in regard to the Soviet Union (as distinct from communism), the French consider and accept it as the dominant power on the Continent. They treat Russia with soberness and dignity, as befits a great nation. There is, in France, none of that emotionalism vis-à-vis the Soviet Union that prevails in other stronger and more distant lands. The French know that Russia, whether Tsarist or commissarist, is an essential part of the European Continent and state system. So long as the Russians stay put on their side of the fence, Frenchmen feel no hostility for them.

But the existence of a large Communist Party inside of France is a different matter. It changes the whole complexion of politics and mitigates against policies that might be sharp and decisive. It also serves as a constant potential danger to any positive action that the French government might take which the Communists would consider hostile to Russia.

For the Communist Party polls about one-fourth of the total vote in France in practically every election. It has a powerful delegation of 101 members in Parliament. Communists are also in control of up to 70 percent of the trade unions, notably in the basic industries, such as transportation, public utilities, metals, and mining. Altogether the highly disciplined Communists form the strongest single political party in France and constitute a major force in the Republic, helping to keep the latter off balance. They are also a strong element in the neutralist movement.

Irving Brown, European representative of the American Federation of Labor, writes:[90]

> The greatest contributing factor in France's internal weakness is the continued domination of its trade-union movement by the Communist-run General Confederation of Labor [C. G. T.]. This provides the Cominform with 50,000 cadres entrenched in the most strategic industries in the country—a formidable machine when one considers that Stalin reportedly once said that, with 150,000 party organization secretaries, he ruled the U. S. S. R. . . .
>
> Much of French "neutralism," or rather "defeatism," . . . springs from the average worker's lack of faith in the capacity of the Government and the democratic parties to crack the disciplined Communist party if and when the Red Army should strike. This fear explains why millions of workers, who long ago quit the CGT, have not become affiliated with the non-Communist trade unions.

It must, however, be pointed out that the Communist Party has been declining in numbers, if not in influence, ever since May 1947, when its members were ousted from the French cabinet. Membership in the Party itself declined from over 900,000 in 1951 to around 600,000 at the end of 1952. The Communists still continue to poll more than 5,000,000 votes, but their percentage has decreased from 28.6 percent of the total in 1946 to 24.8 percent in 1951. Their appeals for political strikes have fallen on deaf ears, even among those workers who vote Communist.

Nevertheless, the Communists are still France's largest single political force. The 600,000 Party members are a hard core of militants—a potentially dedicated secret army, in the service of the Kremlin, the equivalent of fifty divisions! Propaganda-wise, their influence, direct and indirect, remains potent. It is, therefore, important to know something about what these Communist voters think and believe.

A recent survey carried out by the French magazine Realities through the French Institute of Public Opinion throws a much-needed light on this subject. Thanks to the poll, we can now begin to answer the perplexing question: What makes a Communist in France, and "Why Five Million Frenchmen Vote Communist?" The survey gives us the following composite picture of a French Communist:

1. He comes largely from the ranks of the working class. Of those who said they would vote Communist, 38 percent were factory workers; 8 percent farmhands and white-collar employees each; 5 percent pensioners, civil servants, and tradesmen each; 3 percent professionals; 1 percent executives. 22 percent were housewives.

2. He is relatively young, considerably younger than voters for the other parties; 42 percent of Communist voters are less than thirty-five years old (as against 28 percent of the Gaullists and 11 percent of the Radicals).

3. He is generally a person of no property. Only 18 percent of the Communist voters have their own houses; 11 percent have cars; 3 percent keep servants.

4. He owns a radio set. About 81 percent said that they have radios, a percentage which compares favorably with the rest of the population. This fact is important for propaganda purposes.

What are a French Communist's ideas and demands? Primarily, he wants an improvement in the worker's living conditions and peace. The Communist voter is essentially a pacifist, according to the survey. The report states:

> One of our questions was: "What do you regard as the most important motive for your belief in your party?" Subjects were given a choice of six formulas: wish to see your legitimate interests defended, to work for peace, to associate yourself with those holding the same ideas, to be loyal to your class, to mould the future of France and the world, to see the birth of a happier society. The second formula, "wish to work for peace," was named

as their biggest motive for voting Communist by 32% of those ques-
tioned, as against 28% who put a desire to see their legitimate interests defended first, 19% who gave priority to the birth of a
happier society and only 2% who plumped for class loyalty.

Communist voters tend heavily in the direction of neutralism. To the
question, "Do you think France should take part in a war between the
U.S.S.R. and the U.S.?" 65 percent replied No and only 22 percent said
Yes. The survey also brought out the fact that 60 percent of the Communist
voters believed that the United States was preparing for a war of aggression against the Soviet Union.

Paradoxical as it may sound, French Communists, while generally
anti-American, are not necessarily pro-Soviet. Actually, they are, to a
large extent, indifferent to Russia. Asked which propaganda themes the
Communist Party should stress less, many answered: "Less talk about
Russia." Three quarters of them said that, in case of war, if they would
have to choose between the Soviet Union and peace, they would prefer
peace.

The survey summarizes its findings thus:

> Five million French men and women have chosen the Communist
> party because they were seeking an energetic and dependable cham-
> pion who would help them improve their material lot. Pure poli-
> tics do not interest them. The U.S.S.R., despite a vague sympa-
> thy, gets on their nerves a little. They are ill-informed about
> what is going on in the world, credulous of and confiding in those
> they have once accepted as their oracles . . . They are full of
> faith but not intolerant. They are neutralist, and surprisingly
> enough a majority of them believe in parliamentary institutions
> and democratic liberties.

3. Attitude Toward Germany

The second determining factor in France's European policy today is
deep and continuing distrust and fear of Germany. Despite the adoption
of the Schuman Plan and despite the French government's support of the
institutions of union, the nation as a whole still dreads Germany. Frenchmen do not ignore the possibility of a Communist or Russian victory over
France, but they feel that they are threatened by a greater danger closer
to home. Russia is physically far away and had never invaded France.
Germany is near and had bled France three times in two generations. As
a middle-class Frenchman said to the correspondent of the New York
Times (January 3, 1950): "For us, the Russians are something formidable
but also something distant. But the Germans— ah, they are just over the
border."

The fear of France's Enemy Number One is at present intensified by
the resurgence of German industry and by the American-inspired program

of arming Germans as an integral part of a European army. The idea of Germans in uniform again sends a tremor through France. For the French still nurse bitter historic memories, and they are keenly aware that the Germans, if united, outnumber them nearly two to one.

This passionate dread of Germany was illustrated dramatically early in 1952 in the French Chamber of Deputies. During one of the debates on German rearming, there arose one Georges Heuillard, deputy from the Seine-Inférieure, and dragged himself, with the support of two canes, to the speaker's rostrum. He was obviously dying, his face ashen, scarred, his body crippled and misshapen. There was deathly silence in the Chamber as Heuillard spoke:

> For two years I was in a concentration camp. I saw die all my comrades in the Resistance network. I saw die in Flossenburg almost the entire shipment of prisoners who have come from Buchenwald . . . We have sworn an oath among us that the eventual survivors would never permit Germany to recreate her military strength. Today, despite all these memories, despite all these material and moral ruins still yawning before us, we are about to recreate the German army . . . Is our public opinion ready to accept the consequences? Ask those who were deported or the families of those who did not return . . . Ask the young men who helped to beat down military Germany, the eternal Germany, the Germany of all time!

Heuillard, choking with emotion, swallowed some pills, looked at Foreign Minister Sch man and continued:

> I am going to die, [91] Monsieur le Ministre. I am condemned. My election found me in a surgical clinic . . . I am dying because of the German army. I would not want my sons or my grandsons to be enlisted alongside the tyrants and executioners of their father . . . I have fulfilled my mission. I had promised my comrades to do it. I . . . cry to you: Beware of Germany! Beware of Germany!

The whole Assembly rose to its feet in frenzied applause. Many an eye filled with tears. Heuillard at that moment personified France's deepest emotions. Time magazine, reporting the story [February 25, 1952], concluded:

> The crippled deputy was all but unknown in the National Assembly . . . But his choked emotional voice was, that day . . . the authentic voice of France. Divided on almost everything else, Frenchmen united in fear and hatred of Germany.

4. Neutralism[92]

Much neutralist feeling is still to be found in France, as in the rest of

Western Europe. Part of it is due to a quiet resentment against both global powers which, it is felt, are pushing and cold-bloodedly manipulating Europe for their own power-political or "imperialistic" purposes. Propaganda emanating from Washington and Moscow contributes to maintain a good deal of distrust of both powers. Since each side accuses the other of aggression and warmongering, many Europeans cannot avoid the conclusion that there is a measure of truth in the charges. War talk is, therefore, "in the air," so to speak, and is connected with America as much as with Russia.

The anti-Americans in Europe constitute only a minority, but it is neither a small nor a silent one. In France no less than one fourth (in Italy it is over one third) of the electorate votes the Communist ticket quite consistently. This sizable minority is not necessarily Communist, but it must not be forgotten that much of it is anticapitalist and anti-American. A private survey made in 1952 in France, western Germany, and Italy showed that at least 20 percent of the people would consider the United States guilty in case a new war broke out. However, in the same countries from one third to one half of the respondents said that they would regard the Soviet Union as the culprit. In France around one half of the people expressed no opinion either way.

French neutralism, in so far as it exists and is vocal, also derives from the very real fear that war, any future war, would be fought once more on its soil; and, they insist, two wars in one generation are more than enough. Frenchmen say they could not afford another liberation.

A 1952 poll showed real fears on the part of Frenchmen that their country would become a battlefield in case of another war. In France 59 percent of the people expressed such a dread.

In the same survey the question of how best to avoid war brought out responses that indicated that the current of neutralism still runs fairly strong. A little more than one third of the respondents in France expressed the opinion that a military alliance with the United States would avert war, but a large percentage thought otherwise. Many people came out for disarmament— another form of neutrality— as a means of warding off another possible world conflict, which could only lead, they fear, to the final destruction of Europe. In France 41 percent expressed themselves as favoring the disarmament of Europe as a means of avoiding war.

In France neutralist feeling, which has natural enough causes, is reenforced by Communist propaganda. It is, clearly, to the advantage of the friends of Moscow that Western Europe should remain weak, militarily and otherwise. In supporting a neutral position, Communist propaganda has met with not inconsiderable success among non-Communists, peasants, intellectuals, students. Neutralism is to be found even among Church circles. Many a Churchman considers the present conflict between the United States and the Soviet Union as a struggle between capitalism and communism, both of the latter of which are not looked upon with favor. Communism and capitalism, being basically materialistic, are regarded

with distrust as containing elements of evil. This was revealed in a remarkable letter which four cardinals of France made public on September 8,
1949. It said in part:

> The Church refuses to join a "Crusade" in which are intermixed
> so many temporal and economic rivalries and interests; it knows
> that by doing so it would compromise the purity of its mission
> which is essentially spiritual . . . In condemning the action of the
> Communist parties the Church does not take the part of capitalism.
> It is necessary to know that there exists in the very idea of capital-
> ism . . . a materialism rejected by Christian teaching.

The case for neutralism and its concomitant, political-military neutrality has been cogently stated by one of its leading figures in France,
Hubert Beuve Mery, director of the influential Paris daily Le Monde:[93]

> Europe cannot even hold out against Soviet aggression and will
> be unable to do so for a long time. Accordingly, Europe— with
> England probably excluded— should be neutralized. It should be
> sufficiently armed not to be a freely offered victim, and sufficiently
> disarmed to bar offensive action and the sacrifice of social prog-
> ress and economic stability to military strength. To induce the
> Russians to accept and even guarantee this neutrality, Moscow
> should be assured that Europe and its immediate dependencies will
> not furnish bases or other aid against agression thus made incon-
> ceivable. At the same time Washington could be assured that the
> Europeans, firmly on guard against any extension of the cold war,
> are by no means inclined to move into the opposite camp. A Europe
> that could show the morale of the Finns and Norwegians, the public
> spirit of the English, and the defensive power of the Swedes or
> Swiss would really have nothing to fear from the Russians . . .
>
> A neutral Europe strikes many Europeans as a crazier and
> even more dangerous solution than organic union with the United
> States. In their view, the aggressiveness and drive for expansion
> of the Russians are self-evident and the source of all the trouble.
> But while only a blind or dishonest person can deny that the Soviet
> Union seizes every opportunity to increase its influence in the
> world, it must also be stated that Russia did not attack Greece
> after the failure of General Markos, or Berlin at the time of the
> air lift, or Yugoslavia after its resounding secession, and has
> not crossed Iran's open frontier. Even in Korea it is quite prob-
> able that nothing would have happened if the Americans, two
> years before the war began, had not critically weakened their
> position by giving free rein to the swaggering Syngman Rhee.

5. Opposition to E. D. C.

On May 26, 1952, the French government signed the German Peace

Contract and the European Defense Community (E. D. C.) treaty a day later. The latter, requiring ratification by the six participating European parliaments, has faced particularly bitter opposition throughout France.

E. D. C. is the military umbrella of the six countries that make up the Coal and Steel Community, or Schuman Plan, namely: Belgium, France, Germany, Italy, Luxembourg, and the Netherlands. Although a separate organization, E. D. C. is to be considered an integral part of N. A. T. O., which approved it at its Lisbon meeting in February 1952. E. D. C.'s forces are to consist of basic national units supplied by the member countries. The unit, known as groupment, is to be made up of 12,600 men for the armored forces and 13,000 for the infantry. Integration is to take place at army corps level, each corps to be made up of three or four groupments of different nationality. The ultimate total strength of these forces is to be decided upon by N. A. T. O., which is also to have the authority to dispose of them how and wherever necessary. The latter is one of the provisions to which French leaders and public opinion object with particular vehemence.

In the month following the signature of the E. D. C. treaty, French opinion has tended to become increasingly hostile to it. The idea of Germans in military uniform, and marching side by side with the French, is stirring up widespread fears in France. The dread of a remilitarized Germany[94] is not confined to any one political party but is, as we have seen, shared by the nation as a whole.

France's fears of a rearmed Germany are mixed. Partly they are the conventional dread of a dangerous neighbor that had been ugly in the past; partly they are apprehensions about the future. The French do not share the American optimism about Germany's reliability as an ally. They doubt whether, in a showdown between East and West, the Germans would be found on the side of the democracies. Frenchmen are inclined to assume not. They fear that a remilitarized Germany would find itself in a powerful strategic position to sell its services to the highest bidder. In this area the French suffer from a double apprehension, each contradicting the other. They are troubled by the American tendency to admire the Germans and are worried by the possibility that the Americans, impetuous and impatient with the French "dragging their feet," would make an out-and-out alliance with Germany at the expense of France and the rest of Western Europe. They know that such ideas are entertained in influential German circles. Last November a former General in the Wehrmacht said to an American: "Look, why don't your people and mine get together and really organize an army here? To hell with the French."

On the other hand, Frenchmen fear that the rearmed Germans would make a deal with the Soviet Union. The distrustful French know that such an arrangement might be highly profitable to the Germans, especially the industrialists. Moscow can give the Germans some highly tempting prizes, including long-term and favorable markets not only in Eastern Europe but also in China. It can also, if forced by military necessity to do so, offer the Germans territory long coveted by them, notably the Sudetenland, Austria, and, finally, western Poland. To the French these possibilities are not as far-fetched as they seem. They recall that in the past Germans and Russians had joined at least three times to partition Poland and that in the last thirty years they had combined at least twice in military and political alliances.

Still another reason why so many French look askance at E. D. C. is the fear that the Germans might be tempted to use force to reunite the eastern part of their country with the western. If that should happen, the French are afraid that, as Germany's military allies, they would find themselves in the impossible position of having to fight side by side with their historic enemies for a cause that is not even remotely theirs.

These crosscurrents of dreads, so confusing and contradictory, may sound unrealistic and exaggerated to the outside world, but to the French they are very real. And if West European unity is to be achieved, France's apprehensions must be allayed. This is now one of the tasks, as well as challenges, of the Eisenhower administration.

VI. CONCLUSION

France's attempts to recapture her greatness have been marked by much trial and some error, by a good deal of confusion and considerable self-doubt. Success has been attained here and there. Industrially the nation is better off than at any period since the Germans marched into France. But psychologically and politically there have been no important changes. France as a whole still gropes in the dark and wonders about her future. A clear national policy has not yet emerged, nor national unity, nor vigorous leadership.

The fundamental question is whether a nation situated as France is has any future as a great power; whether she can hope again to be master of her destiny. It is, of course, possible that in a world of superpowers no intermediate nation has much of a chance to play a decisive role. But in so far as such a role is still possible for a middle power, France, to play it, must undergo fundamental changes, particularly in technology and national discipline. She must catch up with the twentieth-century power world as quickly as possible or find herself hopelessly outclassed and outdistanced.

In 1914−18 the French could successfully resist a German assault largely because the two countries were more or less evenly matched in military technology. If Germany had superiority in manpower, France more than made up for it through her allies. In other ways the belligerents had no decisive edge on one another. It was German Pferde against French chevaux, German horse-drawn cannon against French horse-drawn cannon, German bayonets against French bayonets. The result was a trench-war stalemate, until America's fresh and seemingly inexhaustible power broke the deadlock. In 1940, however, the Germans had what the French lacked— a modern technology; it was German planes against French foot soldiers. And the Germans struck where the French were most vulnerable— in their lack of mobility. Technology won, quickly and decisively.

It is clear that unless France transforms herself technologically and achieves flexibility in her whole social-intellectual structure, she will not be able to compete on a basis of equality with the world's modern powers.

The core of the matter is the educational system which, particularly in its upper levels, is exclusive, classical, and rigid. A severe and savage system of examinations excludes all but a select minority from the benefits of technical and higher education. The French system trains many admirable scholars and able scientists, but frustrates them by failing or refusing to provide them with opportunities for jobs or self-expression. This both impoverishes the whole society and breeds intellectual revolt. In their frustration, many educated Frenchmen become Communists or Fascists, or "I don't give a damn-ers" (Je m'en foutistes).

In this connection one of the grave problems is the class basis of the intellectual elite. Although the educational system is free and open to all

86

students, regardless of status or origin, who can pass the examinations, in practice it is largely although by no means exclusively the children of the wealthier people who can attend the universities and professional schools. Offspring of the poor simply cannot afford to acquire a higher education, first because it requires money to support themselves while studying and, second, because the parents usually need the income from their unmarried children's work. It is a matter of astonishment that the French democracy has for decades recruited its professional and educated people from the upper layer of the society and neglected the overwhelming majority of the children of the poor. In 1948—49 only 2 percent of the students in the professional and technical schools came from working class homes, and 7.1 percent from the artisan ranks. The rest, or around 90 percent, were children of the bourgeoisie or professional people.

A program is now under way to provide state scholarships for students from poor homes to enable them to pursue their studies. The time is, indeed, overripe for such a step, particularly in a democracy where, unlike in the United States, there is no general custom or opportunity for students to support themselves while going to college.

An additional difficulty in the French educational system has been the emphasis on the classics, literature, rhetoric, and logic. In a nontechnological age, French humanism was both fruitful and worthy of imitation. It gave France a leading intellectual position and set cultural standards for a large part of the civilized world. Over the years the French came to put an exceedingly high value on literary style and wit, to the comparative neglect of other intellectual values.

Today France is paying heavily for this rich heritage of her literary culture and for this relative neglect of other disciplines. The country must now attempt a reorientation in its individualistic outlook and humanistic education. France, to become a twentieth-century power, will find it necessary to bridge the gap between purely humanist-individualist values and technological-scientific requirements. A modern nation, though it cannot forego the things of the spirit, needs more than the things of the spirit. It needs also the fruit of natural science and engineering. It needs the disciplined insight provided by the social sciences, which are poorly developed in France. It needs, in other words, a combination of an American-type modernism and a French-type humanism. Perhaps France could some day find the golden mean between the two.

APPENDIX A

SELECT BIBLIOGRAPHY IN ENGLISH

This work is based almost entirely on (1) direct observation and experience in France; (2) newspaper accounts; and (3) primary sources, such as surveys, opinion polls, government reports, and special studies. The bibliography listed below is not one which this book drew upon. The author has merely selected a number of books which, in his opinion, will enable the student to gather additional information on France. The following books are scholarly, informative and, if not always up to date, still relevant.

Aglion, R. The Fighting French (1943).
Brogan, D. W. The Development of Modern France, 1870—1939 (1940).
Buthman, W. C. The Rise of Integral Nationalism in France (1939).
Clough, S. B. France: A History of National Economics, 1789—1939 (1939).
Cowan, L. G. France and the Saar, 1680—1948 (1951).
D'Ormesson, V. France (1939).
Earle, E. M. (ed.). Modern France: Problems of the Third and Fourth Republics (1951).
Ehrmann, H. W. French Labor from Popular Front to the Liberation (1947).
Goguel, F. France Under the Fourth Republic (1952).
Guérard, A. J. The France of Tomorrow (1942).
Hale, R. W. Democratic France: The Third Republic from Sedan to Vichy (1941).
MacKay, D. C. The United States and France (1951).
Maurois, A. Why France Fell (1941).
Micaud, C. A. The French Right and Nazi Germany, 1933—39 (1943).
Millar, G. R. Maquis (1945).
Padover, S. K. France: Setting or Rising Star? (1950).
Pertinax. The Grave-Diggers of France (1943).
Pickles, D. M. France Between the Republics (1946).
Priestley, H. I. France Overseas (1938).
Rossi, A. Communist Party in Action (1950).
Spengler, J. J. France Faces Depopulation (1938).
Taylor, O. R. The Fourth Republic of France (1951).
Tissier, P. The Government of Vichy (1942).
Wright, G. Raymond Poincaré and the French Presidency (1942).
Wright, G. The Reshaping of French Democracy (1948).

APPENDIX B

PARTY GROUPS IN THE NATIONAL ASSEMBLY

January 1951		July 1951	
Communists	167	Communists	99
Union of Progressive Republicans	7	Union of Progressive Republicans	4
Affiliated	4		
Triumph of Democratic Liberties in Algeria	3		
African Democratic Rally	6	African Democratic Rally	3
Overseas Independents	11		
Affiliated	1		
Independent Left	3		
Socialists	99	Socialists	105
		Affiliated	2
M.R.P. (Popular Republic Movement)	145	M.R.P.	83
		Affiliated	2
		Overseas Independents (affiliated)	9
Radical Socialists	44	Radical Socialists	66
Affiliated	3	Affiliated	6
U.D.S.R. (Soc. Dem. Resistance Union)	12	U.D.S.R.	14
Affiliated	3	Affiliated	2
		Independent Republicans of	
Peasant and Social Action	19	Peasant and Social Action	34
Affiliated	1	Affiliated	3
Democratic Union of Independents		French Independents (affiliated)	3
(affiliated)	7		
Independent Republicans	24	Independent Republicans	43
Affiliated	1	Affiliated	8
P.R.L. (Republican Liberty Party)	27		
Affiliated	2		
Democratic and Social Action	16	R.P.F. (Rally of the French People)	118
Affiliated	1	Affiliated	3
Independent Popular Republicans			
(affiliated)	6		
Unaffiliated	9	Unaffiliated	19
Total	621	Total	626

90

	1946		1951	
	Deputies	Percentage	Deputies	Percentage
Communists	187	30.5	103	16.5
Socialists	103	16.6	104	16.6
M.R.P.	166	26.9	85	13.6
R.G.R.	65	10.5	94	15.0
Independents and Moderates	73	11.8	98	15.7
R.P.F.	5*	0.8	118	18.8
Miscellaneous Overseas parties	18	2.9	24	3.8
Total	617†		626	

*Candidates elected on the Gaullist Union ticket.

†Upper Volta was represented in the National Assembly by three deputies, in accordance with the law of April 1, 1948.

APPENDIX C

THE VOTE IN THE GENERAL ELECTIONS OF 1946 AND 1951*

Registrations, votes, and abstentions in Metropolitan France in the general elections of November 10, 1946, and of June 17, 1951, were as follows:

	1946	1951
Voters registered	25,052,233	24,973,148
Abstentions	5,487,000 (21.9%)	5,457,790 (21.8%)
Voided ballots	362,163	533,349
Votes cast	19,203,070	18,982,009

The table below lists the votes cast in Metropolitan France on November 10, 1946, and on June 17, 1951, for the large political parties and groups, including their affiliates. The figures given for the R.G.R. include the votes received by the Radical Socialists, the U.D.S.R., and the R.G.R., in districts where these parties presented separate lists. Similarly, the votes received by the P.R.L. and the Peasant Group are included in the figures given for the Independents and Moderates.

	1946		1951		
	Votes	Percentage	Votes	Percentage	Difference
Communists	5,489,288	28.6	5,038,587	26.5	-450,701
Socialists	3,431,954	17.9	2,764,210	14.5	-667,744
M.R.P.	5,058,307	26.4	2,353,544	12.3	-2,704,763
R.G.R.	2,381,384	12.4	2,194,213	11.5	-187,171
Independents)					
Moderates)	2,465,526	12.8	2,496,570	13.1	+31,044
R.P.F.	313,635†	1.6	4,134,885	21.7	+3,821,250
Miscellaneous	62,976	0.3			
	19,203,070		18,982,009		

*From <u>Ambassade de France</u>, Service de Presse, July 16, 1951.
†These votes were cast for Gaullist Union lists.

92

APPENDIX D

FRENCH PREMIERS SINCE 1945*

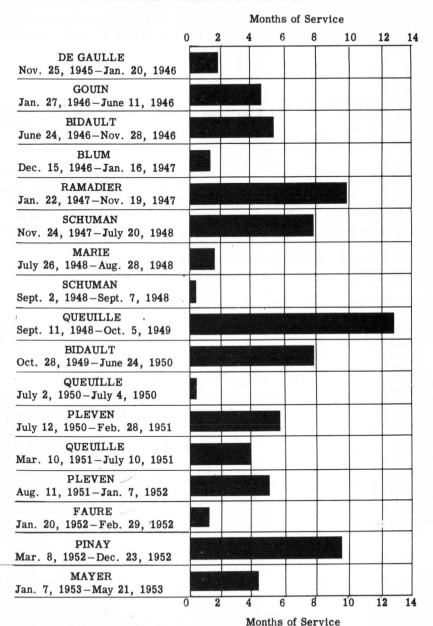

Months of Service

Months of Service

NOTES

1. A. Siegfried, Tableau des partis en France (Paris: Grasset, 1930), p. 199.

2. D. Thomson, Democracy in France. The Third Republic (London: Oxford University Press, 1946), p. 10. ". . . study of the third Republic cannot be divorced from consideration of the whole development of modern France."

3. A. Siegfried, loc. cit., p. 70.

4. A. Siegfried, loc. cit., p. 62.

5. Cited by A. Siegfried, loc. cit., p. 192.

6. D. Thomson, loc. cit., p. 14. "It became customary to think of democracy and government as two separate poles in politics, too far apart for the vital spark of democratic government to flash between them."

7. Alain, Éléments d'une doctrine radicale (Paris: Gallimard, 1925), p. 123.

8. Robert de Jouvenel, La République des Camarades (Paris: Grasset, 1914; rééd. 1934), p. 4.

9. Alain, loc. cit., p. 131.

10. We say neo-Gaullism in order to avoid any confusion between the present political movement of General de Gaulle and the Gaullism of the war years, an entirely national and patriotic movement which included many who now oppose the R. P. F.

11. To be more precise, we use here the two terms "economic democracy" and "social democracy," so as to distinguish more clearly the various aspects of what up to now we have designated by the latter expression.

12. Familles dans le Monde, January–March, 1949.

13. See also Chapter II, Section 3.

14. The employer pays about 40 percent— 10 percent of the salaries for social insurance proper, 17 percent for family allowances, 3 percent for labor accidents, 6 percent for paid vacations.

15. See Section 5 of this chapter.

16. Jean Dayre, "Peut-on améliorer le rendement national?" in Cahiers Français d'Information, March 15, 1948.

17. This is, of course, not much compared to the American automobile industry, which produces well over 6 billion cars and trucks annually.

18. L'Étrange Défaite is the title of a book by the Sorbonne professor, Marc Bloch, who was assassinated by the Nazis in June 1944. The book was published posthumously in 1946.

19. These included: 7 capital ships, 2 aircraft carriers, 19 cruisers, 70 destroyers, and 77 submarines. Much of this fleet was to be sunk later by the French themselves to keep it out of British and, later, German hands.

20. See R. Jacomet (Contrôleur Général de l'Armée), L'Armement de la France, 1936–39 (Paris, 1945).

21. In the levée en masse decreed by the Revolutionary government on August 23, 1792: "The young men shall go to battle; the married men shall forge arms and transport provisions; the women shall make tents and clothing, and shall serve in the hospitals; the children shall turn old linen into lint; the aged shall betake themselves to the public places in order to rouse the courage of the warriors and preach hatred of kings and the unity of the Republic."

22. "C'est ce sentiment de la superiorité morale qui, précisément, donne à l'Armée française la certitude de la victoire. . . . L'instinct collectif chez l'Allemand est ressenti comme l'oppression d'une masse immense, force obscure

qui s'impose à chacun et lui enlève toute volonté propre. . . . Le Français, au contraire, ne se sent vraiment à l'aise collectivement que dans des réunions d'hommes restreintes, dont les individus lui sont connus, il supporte la discipline collective, non comme une force de coercition mais comme une limitation consentie."— La France Militaire, Centre d'Informations Documentaires (Paris, 1940), p. 240.

23. Lt. Col. F. Vandaele, "L'Armée belge au Canal Albert," Revue de Défense Nationale, June 1948. The Belgian forces consisted of 18 infantry divisions, 2 chasseur divisions, 1 corps of cavalry with 2 motorized divisions, 2 regiments of cyclists, 2 regiments of fort artillery, 1 brigade of field artillery, 2 antiaircraft regiments, 3 aviation regiments.

24. But on June 4, in the ruins of Dunkirk, the Germans captured 80,000 French. See A. Zevaès, Histoire de Six Ans 1938–1944 (Paris, 1944), p. 82.

25. See R. Céré, La seconde guerre mondiale (Paris, 1947); A. Schwob, L'Affaire Pétain (édition de la Maison Française, 1944).

26. Many of these individual units, though cut off from any central command, continued to fight heroically but without hope. See, for example, the story of Pierre Keller (Général de division), La division de Metz, 42 D.I., pendant la bataille de France (Paris, 1947); Commandant N. Bourin, Le second drame de Maubeuge, (Paris, 1947); General de la Laurencie, Les opérations du IIIe Corps d'Armée (Paris, 1947). See also Col. de Bardies, La campagne 1939–1940, and General Doumenc, Dunkerque et la campagne de Flandre (Paris, 1947). All these are, of course, written by interested parties and should be read with caution.

27. Among the patriots who were prevented from escaping and who paid with their lives was the Minister of Interior Georges Mandel. For studies of this remarkable man, see P. Coblentz, Georges Mandel (Paris, 1946); G. Suarez, Nos seigneurs et maîtres (Paris, 1937); P. Carrère, Profils (Paris, 1937); P. Morel, Les grands hommes de l'Union Nationale. Mandel did manage to go to North Africa to organize a resistance there, but the Pétainists brought him back and delivered him to the Germans who, in turn, handed him over to the French fascist miliciens who murdered him on July 7, 1944.

28. A day later another French general, Charles de Gaulle, whose book on mechanized warfare, Vers l'Armée de Métier (Paris, 1934), was ignored by the French High Command but not by the Germans, spoke different words. Addressing the French people from London, whither he had escaped, he said: "Has the last word been said? No! The same means which have vanquished us can some day bring us victory. Struck today by a mechanical force, we can in the future win with a superior mechanical force. The destiny of the world lies there."

29. Of all the major fronts on which the Germans fought in World War II, the one of France in 1940 was the least costly in casualties. See Saul K. Padover: Experiment in Germany (New York: Duell, Sloan and Pearce, 1946), pp. 266–69; "Was Germany Beaten?". . Toronto Star Weekly, April 6, 1946; "Is Germany Really Kaput?" Science Digest, May 1946.

30. In a French public opinion poll concerning the weakness of France in 1939, 31 percent held the people responsible, 18 percent the politicans, 13 percent politics, 8 percent treason, 8 percent national disunity, 8 percent low birth rate. See Sondage de l'Opinion Publique française, June 15, 1945.

31. See General de Cugnac, Les quarante jours (Paris, 1947). For a critique of the "extrème faiblesse du commandement," see Col. de Bardies, La campagne 1939–1940 (Paris, 1947).

32. "La défaite de 1940 a son origine moins dans notre infériorité du moment

en moyens matériels que dans une éclipse de la pensée militaire française durant les vingt années qui se sont écoulées entre les deux conflits mondiaux."— T. Albord, "Appel à l'Imagination," Revue de défense nationale, August–September 1949.

33. See Giraud's memoirs, Un seul but: la Victoire (Paris, 1949). The New York Herald Tribune (Paris ed., July 6, 1949) reviewer wrote of Giraud: "At heart he agreed with Pétain in many things, notably in maintaining a firm, disciplined patriarchal society in France."   .

34. For a sympathetic biography of Pétain, see the book by his Directeur du Cabinet, Jean Tracou: Le Maréchal aux Liens (Paris, 1949).

35. Listed in the anti-Semitic sheet La Libre Parole, Dec. 19, 1898.

36. Colonel Henry confessed the forgery, was arrested, and committed suicide. See F. Goguel, La Politique des Partis sous la IIIe République (Paris, 1946), p. 92.

37. On May 25, 1940, a month before Pétain asked for an armistice and while France still had her main forces intact, Weygand complained: "La France a commis l'immense erreur d'entrer en guerre n'ayant ni le matériel qu'il fallait, ni la doctrine militaire qu'il fallait."— Les Documents secrets de l'État-Général Français, p. 140; Bloch, op. cit., p. 45.

38. This incident took place at Cangey, on June 11, during a cabinet meeting at which Weygand was present. He said: "Je suis en mesure d'apprendre au Conseil qu'une émeute communiste va éclater à Paris. M. Thorez est arrivé, et, ce soir, monsieur le Président, il couchera à l'Elysée." Mandel, in charge of police and security, replied promptly: "Je suis obligé de répondre au généralissime que les renseignements qu'il vient de nous fournir sont absolument inexacts." Weygand: "Douteriez-vous de ma parole?" Mandel: "Il ne s'agit point de votre parole; mais ma source de renseignements est supérieure à la votre. J'ai eu, il y a à peine quelques minutes, une conversation téléphonique avec M. le préfet de police Langeron, et celui-ci m'a dit qu'en dépit de la gravité de l'heure, la population parisienne fait preuve d'un calme admirable. Au reste, il est aisé d'en avoir la confirmation immédiate: il suffit d'appeler au téléphone M. Langeron et M. Le Président de la République tiendra la recepteur afin qu'on ne puisse pas douter de la parole d'un civil." This was done, and, while Weygand sat in silence, the Police Prefect of Paris confirmed by telephone that the capital was calm and that there was no sign of Communist activity.

39. Anti-British feeling existed also among the generals. When Giraud, for example, was spirited out of France in a submarine, the first question he asked was whether it was British or American; if British, he said, he would not care to set foot in it. (Personal conversation with the submarine commander.)

40. At least three admirals were later condemned by French courts: Admiral Platon was executed in 1944; Admiral de Laborde was condemned to death but his sentence was commuted to life imprisonment; Admiral Esteva is now in perpetual detention.

41. Cot, Triumph of Treason (Chicago: Ziff-Davis, 1944).

42. Darnand was a professional criminal who, under Vichy, became chief of the Fascist militia. "Darnand . . . est un ancien cagoulard, mais il est surtout un bandit. Compromis dans des affaires d'assassinat, entrepreneur louche de transport, il avait à la préfecture de Police un dossier spécialement chargé."— Raymond Aron, De L'Armistice à l'Insurrection Nationale (Paris, 1945), p. 337.

43. Juenger's diary, in German, was serialized in a Swiss journal in 1949.

44. On July 30, 1940, Pétain set up a Cour Suprème de Justice to try men like Blum, Daladier, Gamelin, etc., in order to discredit the Republic. This

led to the famous Riom trial, which boomeranged against the Pétainists. As the Nazi _Pariser_ _Zeitung_ (April 3, 1942) remarked ironically: "The French Generals have been no more successful in the court than in the field. "

45. Forces Françaises Intérieures, the group name of the French army of Resistance.

46. "En fait, la France entière avait commercé avec l'ennemi et la classe ouvrière n'avait pu subsister qu'en se mettant à la solde de l'ennemi. À ce sujet une sorte de compromis fut tacitement conclu entre gaullistes et communistes, chacun défendant sa clientèle. Les uns ne reprocheraient pas aux ouvriers d'avoir consciencieusement fignolé pendant quatre ans des camions et des tanks pour les 'boches'; les autres ne poursuivraient pas à boulets rouges les grands industriels qui avaient gagné des milliards, grâce au travail des ouvriers. " J. Galtier-Boissière, Histoire de la Guerre 1939−1945, Vol. V, p. 391.

47. Ibid. "De tous les hauts militaires poursuivis, aucun n'a été fusillé. . . . Ni un gros industriel, ni un général, ni un magistrat ne serait envoyé au poteau. "

48. This number does not include the "Reign of Terror" instituted by the Communists in the summer and autumn of 1944. How many people were murdered by them and by the criminals who infiltrated the ranks of the Resistance, is not certain. The figures given vary from 80,000 to 100,000, but this is probably an exaggeration. See American Mercury, April 1946; a letter in Aux Écoutes, February 28, 1947; La Révolution Proletarienne, August 1947. All that can be said for sure is that several thousand people were killed without trial.

49. Of these, 2,777 were condemned to perpetual forced labor; 10,434 to a specified period of forced labor; 2,713 to confinement.

50. See Figaro, April 29, 1949.

51. Carlton J. H. Hayes, France A Nation of Patriots (New York: Columbia University Press, 1930). There is now a need for a clarifying analysis between patriotism and class identification. Numerous Frenchmen who collaborated with the Nazis unquestionably did so for reasons that seemed to them to be sincerely patriotic; the same can be said for those who killed their compatriots because they collaborated with the enemy. Under these circumstances the whole concept of "patriotism" obviously requires investigation.

52. One must mention a number of other leading individuals sentenced by various courts: Henri Beraud, writer; Bernard Faÿ, historian and former curator of the Bibliothèque, who denounced fellow-Frenchmen to the Nazis as Freemasons; Stephane Lauzanne, former editor-in-chief of the newspaper Matin; Charles Maurras, director of Action Française and member of the French Academy; Robert Brasillach, editor of Je Suis Partout and a poet, shot on Feb. 6, 1945; Gaston Bergery, former ambassador to Turkey; Louis Auphan, an editor of Action Française, condemned by the Cour de Justice of Lyon to twenty years of hard labor; Jean Lousteau, speaker on Radio Paris, condemned to death on Nov. 30, 1945; Abel Hermant, author, condemned to life imprisonment on Dec. 15, 1945; Comte Armand de Chastenet de Puysegur, condemned to death in Oct. 1944, sentence commuted to life imprisonment on Dec. 19, 1945; Guy Bunau-Varilla, political editor of Matin, condemned for life in 1946; Jean Luchaire, editor, condemned to death in 1946; Michel Detroyat, aviator, condemned to national degradation for life in 1946; Robert Peyronnet, radio producer, condemned to twenty years hard labor in 1946; Jean Berthelot, minister under Laval, condemned to two years and national degradation; Hubert Lagardelle, another Laval minister, condemned to forced labor for life; Cayla, former governor of Madagascar, condemned to five years; Amédée Bussiere, prefect of police of Paris, condemned to forced labor for life; Admiral Auphan, for his

role in the scuttling of the fleet at Toulon on Nov. 27, 1942, condemned to forced labor for life, but in absentia.

53. See also Chapter II, Section 1.

54. "Le mouvement de concentration technique industrielle ne s'est pas poursuivi en France à un rythme aussi rapide qu'à l'étranger. . . . Ce faible dégrê de concentration se traduit par l'usage réduit de la force motrice puisque 74.5% des établissements français ne sont pas dotés de la force motrice." J. Hardy, La Crise Française (Paris, 1945), p. 198.

55. See General Dejussieu-Pontcarral, La Nation armée de la République Française (Paris, 1948).

56. A French intelligence report of Jan. 26, 1940, listed the Luftwaffe as having 5,150 planes of the line, of which 1,250 were fighters and about 2,500 bombers. Another 6,900 were in stock or in use by the aviation schools.

57. "Lorsq'un avion sort d'usine, il est soumis à des essais de réception en vol. Tant que cet avion n'a pas été receptionné, il appartient au constructeur. Au contraire, après réception, il appartient à l'État. C'est alors un avion pris en compte." For the whole account, see P. Lyet and Lt. Col. de Cossé-Brissac, "Combien d'Avions Allemands contre combien d'Avions Français le mai 1940?" Revue de défense nationale, June 1948.

58. General Gamelin reported to him that, though German superiority in bombers was in proportion of 2.3 to 1, nevertheless the French and British aviation together were "en mesure, toute-fois, d'infliger des pertes telles à l'ennemi que celui-ci soit amenê à renoncer en partie aux attaques de jour." There was no ground whatever, either in the known tactics or in the known figures, for such an assumption.

59. See Colonel Ferré, Le défaut de l'Armure (Paris, 1949).

60. The bravery and skill of the French pilots were beyond question. In about forty days of combat they made 10,000 sorties and carried off 814 victories; but in the first three days of the blitz they lost 179 machines, almost half of the available craft. A total of 166 pilots, more than one-third of the total, were killed in action. See Lt. Col. Salesse, L'Aviation de chasse française en 1939–1940 (Paris, 1949); P. Paquier (ed.), Les forces aériennes françaises de 1939 à 1945 (Paris, 1949).

61. The French craft had a speed of 450 km. per hour, as against 550 km. of the German planes; in addition, 429 of them (and two days later, only 323) had to face 1,500 German machines. In bombers the French were outnumbered thirty-five to one.

62. In this respect there have been some changes since the Liberation. Not only were a number of underground leaders, whose record was heroic, incorporated into the regular French Army as officers (despite the strong protest of the professionals), but there is now evidence of the realization that a democratic society has certain moral obligation to its soldiers. On May 27, 1949 Le Monde Militaire published a remarkable statement to this effect by X. Louis, Chaplain of the Invalides. He wrote: "Mon expérience de quatre années d'aumonier militaire m'amène à certifier que la cause la plus profonde de l'antimilitarisme d'une notable fraction de la nation réside dans l'irrespect de la dignité humaine. Le plus souvent, de la part des cadres de carrière, ce manque de respect est inconscient et non coupable: ce qui est d'autant plus grave. . . . Un chef doit avoir le souci du bien-être, de la santé, du moral de tous ceux dont il a la charge. Mais il doit avoir le souci majeur de leur dignité. . . . Le devoir le plus essentiel du chef vis-à-vis de ses subordonnés est, dans l'exercice même du commandement, de reconnaître leur valeur d'hommes. . . . Un mot maladroit,

un manque d'égards, une expression dure ou méprisante peuvent sèmer au-
jourd'hui une rancune qui levera demain en clore. . . . Une injure dans la bouche
d'un chef le déshonore et ouvre dans l'âme de l'inférieur une blessure inguéris-
sable. ''

63. To remind oneself of this, one only has to look at some of the great monu-
ments, such as the Arc de Triomphe and the Vendome column, in Paris. The
Latin inscription on the latter, a monument to Napoleon's Bella Germanica in
1805, has a magnificent sound of old-Roman triumph: TRIMESTRI SPATIO
DUCTU SUO PROFLIGATI EX AERE CAPTO GLORIAE EXERCITUS MAXIMI
DICAVIT. As a comment on the vanity of all such efforts, one may remark that
135 years later it took Hitler considerably less than a trimestri to achieve his
triumph in France.

64. At Bir-Hakeim in North Africa, May – June 1942, the French showed
what they could really achieve when their fighting spirit was aroused. There the
First Brigade of the Free French, commanded by General Koenig, dug in and
held off the combined attacks of Italian tanks, Rommel's Panzers, and concentrated Stuka bombers. At a loss of 900 of their own men, they inflicted heavy
damage on the Axis, and finally retired with two-thirds of their effectives, including the wounded, part of their matériel and 300 German and Italian prisoners.

65. See Le Monde, April 27 and 28, 1949; France-Soir, April 28, 1949.

66. See L'Armistice 12 – 16 juin 1940 (Témoignages et textes), ed. by Vexin
(Édition de Minuit: Paris, 1944), which raises the question of the absence of
self-criticism in France and asks why, four years after the armistice, so many
French still ignore the causes of the defeat.

67. Professor Bloch's conclusion is that France's regeneration must come
through the youth. ''La France d'un nouveau printemps devra être la chose des
jeunes. . . . Je n'aurai pas l'outrecuidance de leur tracer un programme. Ils
en tireront eux-mêmes les lois du fond de leur cerveau et de leur cœur. ''—
Op. cit. , p. 191.

68. New York: Éditions de la Maison Française, 1941.

69. ''C'était d'ailleurs les femmes qui paraissaient éprouver la douleur la
plus profonde en face de la capitulation. . . . Les hommes cherchaient un
dérivatif. Ils le trouvaient dans de méchantes accusations: c'est la faute à
Blum. . . . La faute aux chefs de l'Armée. . . .''—Ibid., p. 276.

''Les prêtres disposant de l'unique tribune en France accusaient la vie facile
d'avant guerre; le rélachement des moeurs, voir le divorce, d'être les causes
de la catastrophe, penitence infligée par Dieu. ''— Ibid. , p. 281.

70. Paris, 1945.

71. ''Les responsabilités de toutes ces erreurs doivent certainement être
imputées à l'esprit théorique et peu réaliste des principaux chefs de l'Armée,
toujours bornés aux méthodes de 1914. ''— Ibid. , p. 135.

72. Angoulême, 1941.

73. ''Le grand coupable, nous le designons du doigt, c'est M. Albert Lebrun''
[the man whom Laval and the collaborationists forced to resign!]. —Ibid. , p. 52.

74. Published at Avignon (Aubanel Père), undated.

75. Published at Clermont-Ferrand, 1940. Typical extracts: ''Les institutions
ont corrompu les hommes; il faut changer les institutions. Mais les hommes
ont aussi corrompu les institutions; il faut changer les hommes'' (Xavier Vallat).
''Le plus grand crime qui ait été commis dans notre pays depuis longtemps, est
certainement celui d'avoir déclaré la guerre'' (Laval). ''Si ce pays est descendu
au point où il est tombé.. . . il le doit à une décadence généralisée et il faut

attribuer la responsabilité à cette éducation affreuse de l'opinion publique qui lui a été faite par la presse, par la radio et par le système d'information. . . . C'est l'argent qui a tout corrumpu'' (Flandin).

76. For a plaidoyer of the French episcopate, see Msgr. Guerry (Archbishop of Cambrai and Secretary of the Assembly of Cardinals and Archbishops of France), L'Église Catholique en France sous l'Occupation (Paris, 1947).

77. See Henri Noguères, La République Accuse (Paris, 1945); François and Georges Bourgin, Les Démocraties Contre le Fascisme (Paris, 1946); and Léon Blum, L'Histoire Jugera (Montreal and Paris, 1945), which contains articles and utterances by him from 1932 to 1942, the most important of which are his statements before the Riom court in February and March 1942, during which, in effect, the Socialist leader turned tables on his Vichyite accusers. In general, Socialist defensiveness is due to the fact that many important members of their party held ministerial posts in the government up to 1939, and hence they bear a share of the total responsibility.

78. See the typical Communist line in Florimond Bonté, Le Chemin de l'Honneur (Paris, 1948). "Notre pays connaît les terribles conséquences de la politique criminelle suivie par des gouvernements indignes, responsables de la défaite et de l'occupation. . . . Situons les responsabilités: la clique des dirigeants"—a tract written by Thorez and Duclos, cited on p. 388.

79. Aron, Précis de l'Unité Française (Paris, 1945). In 1939, he writes, there was a kind of general decay; words took the place of action; everyone was concerned only with himself, his own career: "plus de culture, plus d'initiative, plus d'audace, plus de souci de l'État, ni de sens de la continuité du régime ou de la permanence française."—p. 31. See also Schumann, Honneur et Patri (Paris, 1946).

80. C. L. Flavian, De la Nuit vers la Lumière (Paris, 1946), p. 17.

81. Gen. Prioux, Souvenirs de Guerre 1939–1943 (Paris, 1947), p. 156.

82. Pierre Lyet, La Bataille de France Mai–Juin 1940 (Paris, 1947), p. 149. In connection with the Maginot Line troops, Lyet writes: "Des milliers d'hommes dont les chefs refusent de se rendre le 26 juin ne s'inclinent que devant l'ordre formel du Général Huntziger, chef de la délégation francaise d'armistice, mais d'énergiques protestations accompagnent cette reddition d'ouvrages fortifiés invaincus, contraire à toute tradition militaire."

83. Pierre Audiat, Paris pendant la Guerre (Paris, 1946), p. 17.

84. Francis Ambrière, Les Grandes Vacances 1939–1945 (Paris, 1946), p. 63.

85. Marc Leproux, Nous les Terroristes (Monte Carlo, 1947), p. 5. Describing the general confusion, he writes: "Les gens répètent: 'Il faut faire quelque chose,' sans savoir quoi faire. . . . La foule se porte aux concerts ou aux parades données sur les places publiques. Mais il est vrai qu'un bon nombre de personnes se rendent la comme on va au cirque."

86. Sondage de l'Opinion Publique Française.

87. Ibid.

88. This and the subsequent statements are based upon prolonged interviews carried on by my assistant, Fleury Peyrachon, in the summer of 1949 in Paris.

89. This respondent claimed that he was completely unpolitical and that he had never belonged to any political party.

90. New Leader, January 28, 1952.

91. He has since died.

92. For a penetrating analysis of the inner meaning of neutralism, see Daniel

Lerner, "International Coalitions and Communications Contents," in Public Opinion Quarterly, Winter, 1952–53, pp. 681–88.

93. The Nation, August 16, 1952.
94. See Section 3.

THE HOOVER INSTITUTE STUDIES

These studies undertake to describe the world revolution of our time and its consequences for world politics and national policy. They were conducted by the Hoover Institute and Library on War, Revolution, and Peace.

The basic studies appear in five series:

Series A. General: This series contains an introduction to the entire project and several independent studies growing out of the larger research task.

Series B . Elites: A series of studies describing changes in the composition of ruling groups in various countries from 1890 to the present. These studies show the pattern of differences and similarities which we regard as the social process characterizing the world revolution of our time.

Series C. Symbols: A series of studies describing ideological trends and changes in political vocabulary from 1890 to the present.

Series D. Communities: A series of studies portraying in integrated fashion the structure and functioning of communities in various parts of the world. The communities in which people live are of various scopes—and so will be the studies, which range from one of a small peasant village to one of a national community, and perhaps some day, of a world community.

Series E. Institutions: This series will focus on the organization and operation of specific institutions in various countries —such institutions as the factory, the press, the school.

HOOVER INSTITUTE STUDIES

Series A: General

1. The World Revolution of Our Time: A Framework for Basic Policy Research

   This volume is an introduction to the entire program of studies.

   (Other titles to be announced)

Series B: Elites

1. The Comparative Study of Elites: An Introduction and Bibliography
2. The Politburo
3. The Nazi Elite
4. The German Executive: 1890–1933
8. Kuomintang and Chinese Communist Elites

   (Other titles to be announced)

Series C: Symbols

1. The Comparative Study of Symbols: An Introduction
2. The "Prestige Papers": A Survey of Their Editorials
3. Symbols of Internationalism
4. Symbols of Democracy

   In preparation:
5. Symbols of Freedom
6. Symbols of Doctrine
7. The French Ideological Struggle: Political Symbols in Postwar France

   (Other titles to be announced)

Series D: Communities

1. Themes in French Culture: A Preface to a Study of French Community

Series E: Institutions

1. Soviet Economic Institutions: The Social Structure of Production Units
2. French Institutions: Values and Politics

(Other titles to be announced)

Also THE POLICY SCIENCES: RECENT DEVELOPMENTS IN SCOPE AND METHOD. Daniel Lerner and Harold D. Lasswell, editors. Seventeen distinguished social scientists collaborate to present the scientific foundations for research leading to sound national policies.

MOSCOW AND CHINESE COMMUNISTS. Robert C. North. The communist movement in China, its relations with Moscow, and implications of the People's Republic of China.